Social Studies
Instruction
Incorporating the
Language Arts

Social Studies Instruction Incorporating the Language Arts

JOYANN HAUGE MORIN

California State University, Los Angeles

Boston   New York   San Francisco

Mexico City   Montreal   Toronto   London   Madrid   Munich   Paris

Hong Kong   Singapore   Tokyo   Cape Town   Sydney

Executive Editor: Stephen D. Dragin
Series Editor: Traci Mueller
Series Editorial Assistant: Erica Tromblay
Executive Marketing Manager: Amy Cronin Jordan
Production Administrator: Annette Pagliaro
Editorial Production: Walsh & Associates, Inc.
Composition Buyer: Linda Cox
Manufacturing Buyer: Andrew Turso
Cover Administrator: Kristina Mose-Libon
Text Design and Composition: Publishers' Design & Production Services, Inc.

For related titles and support materials, visit our online catalog at
www.ablongman.com

Between the time Website information is gathered and then published, it is not unusual for some sites to have closed. Also, the transcription of URLs can result in unintended typographical errors. The publisher would appreciate notification where these occur so that they may be corrected in subsequent editions.

Library of Congress Cataloging-in-Publication Data

Morin, JoyAnn Hauge.
    Social studies instruction incorporating the language arts / JoyAnn
Hauge Morin.
        p. cm.
    Includes bibliographical references and index.
    ISBN 0-205-37611-8
    1. Social sciences—Study and teaching (Elementary)—California   2.
Language arts (Elementary)—California   3. Lesson planning—California
4. Interdisciplinary approach in education—California.   I. Title.
LB1584.M77 2003
372.83—dc21

                                                            2002071713

Printed in the United States of America
10   9   8   7   6   5   4   3   2   1   07   06   05   04   03   02

This book is dedicated to my husband, Dale Morin, my son, David Morin, my daughter, Angelique Morin, my mother, Anna Hauge, and to the memory of my father, Harry Hauge

Contents

Introduction

Historically, social studies instruction has been based on state- or district-adopted textbooks that guide teachers in planning activities that consider content and sequence appropriate for specific grade levels. An excellent selection of "how-to-teach" textbooks is readily available to provide pre-service as well as experienced teachers with general ideas/strategies related to the teaching of social studies in elementary grades. Most often, prospective teachers are exposed to a multitude of effective teaching practices in a carefully selected, well-written textbook focusing on course-specific content. However, what is not readily available is a series of lesson plans that can be used as models for the development of suggested grade-level topics. This supplemental book builds on that basic knowledge by providing pre-service teachers with an excellent background for the subsequent lesson- and unit-planning tasks. It facilitates planning by providing lesson examples and teaching strategies that illustrate the sequential development of a unit of study appropriate for a specific grade level. The lesson and unit ideas in this book are based on both national and state suggestions.

Conversations with experienced teachers as well as with district personnel have convinced me that they too would welcome a supplement that provides ideas for additional activities to enhance the content found in state- or district-adopted textbooks.

Organization of This Book

This introduction is followed by chapters that illustrate example social studies units, activities, and recommended content for elementary grades 1 through 6.

Additional unit suggestions are included to provide teachers guidance when developing subsequent units related to each grade level. The content is based on the general curriculum standards set forth by the National Council for the Social Studies (NCSS, 1994), and on grade-level content appropriate for designated grade levels.

Inclusion of National Council of Social Studies and State Standards

In 1994, the National Council of Social Studies published a set of curriculum standards to "assure that . . . an integrated social science, behavioral science, and humanities approach for achieving academic and civic competence was available to guide social studies decision makers in K–12 schools in the United States." Recognizing that each state makes specific content, scope, and sequence decisions, these standards were meant "to be used as guides and criteria to establish integrated state, school, department, and classroom curriculum plans to guide instruction and assessment" (p. vii).

These broad standards include suggestions that are readily adaptable as teachers begin to develop and implement related specific state and district requirements. The examples included are based on the goals and curriculum strands set forth in the Curriculum Standards for Social Studies (Bulletin 89, 1994) as well as in specific state- and district-developed social studies frameworks. As indicated by the National Council for Social Studies, the included examples are intended to be used as guides to establish specific state, school, or district curriculum and instruction.

The curriculum standards for social studies served as a starting point for the development of the example units represented in this book. These units were field-tested in coursework focusing on teaching social studies curriculum and instruction. The enrolled pre- and in-service teachers enthusiastically accepted the unit examples as being very useful in the development of subsequent units in their classrooms. The standards are expressed in the following thematic statements (National Council for the Social Studies, Bulletin 89, 1994):

1. *Culture*: Social studies programs should include experiences that provide for the study of culture and cultural diversity.
2. *Time, Continuity, and Change*: Social studies should include experiences that provide for the ways human beings view themselves in and over time.
3. *People, Places, and Environments*: Social studies programs should provide experiences that provide for the study of people, places, and environments.
4. *Individual Development and Identity*: Social studies programs should include experiences that provide for the study of individual development and identity.
5. *Individuals, Groups, and Institutions*: Social studies programs should include experiences that provide for the study of interactions among individuals, groups, and institutions.
6. *Power, Authority, and Governance*: Social studies programs should include experiences that provide for the study of how people create and change structure of power, authority, and governance.
7. *Production, Distribution, and Consumption*: Social studies programs should include experiences that provide for the study of how people organize for the production, distribution, and consumption of goods and services.
8. *Science, Technology, and Society*: Social studies programs should include experiences that provide for the study of relationships among science, technology, and society.
9. *Global Connections*: Social studies programs should include experiences that provide for the study of global connections and interdependence.
10. *Civic Ideals and Practices:* Social studies programs should include experiences that provide for the study of ideals, principles, and practices of citizenship in a democratic republic. (National Council for the Social Studies, 1994, Bulletin 89, pp. 21–31)

Strategies and Techniques

The NCSS standards, as well as the goals and curriculum suggested in most state and district frameworks, encourage teachers to utilize a variety of strategies to provide meaningful instruction that enhances student understanding of history, its causes, and its effects. This book is intended to provide ideas characteristic of effective social studies instruction. The NCSS identified the key features of ideal social studies teaching and learning. In its position statement, these features are summed up in the statement that "*social studies and learning are powerful when they are meaningful, integrative, value-based, challenging, and active*" (NCSS, Bulletin 89, p. 162).

The ideas in this text expand on the standards set forth by State Departments of Education as well as the NCSS Standards. The unit examples for each grade level illustrate an integrated approach to teaching social studies content in an effort to elicit and maintain student interest and active participation and promote an in-depth understanding of historical content. Every effort has been made to provide students with a variety of experiences to enhance the way in which they learn content and develop skills related to the primary purpose of social studies, which "is to help young people develop the ability to make informed and reasoned decisions for the public good as citizens of a culturally diverse, democratic society in an independent world" (NCSS, p. vii).

Models of Teaching

The example units in this book include strategies intended to maximize students' learning. Research has provided a wealth of knowledge that can be applied to encourage the use of a repertoire of teaching models appropriate for the subject matter and the diverse student population for which it is intended (Joyce & Weil, 1980).

The lessons in this book provide teachers with ideas that consider a variety of activities to actively involve the students in their learning. These meaningful experiences provide opportunities for students to gain content knowledge and become involved in an integrated approach in which they learn basic skills, become active participants in their learning, and share in an environment conducive to eliciting and maintaining interest.

Although the focus is on social studies curriculum, the example activities provide learning experiences that include the reinforcement of language arts skills. The learning experiences include direct teaching strategies (one example format is provided on page 17), group activities, the use of drama, and activities that encourage student interaction. Resources for related literature, videocassettes, and computer programs are provided for selected topics.

Literature as a Vehicle to Teach Social Studies

This book utilizes literature as an avenue to bring realism to the people and events in history, a major trend in social studies instruction especially relating to the period of time studied. According to Frederick Risinger's review of contemporary research, curriculum guides, and other reports, this trend continues (1992). Risinger states, "This trend has particular implications for elementary social studies. . . . . Student interest is heightened when literature is used as an integral part of a social studies program. . . . [C]arefully selected literature can make periods come to life and provide a flavor of the thoughts and feeling surrounding a historical event" (p. 2).

When Charlotte Crabtree (1989) wrote about the power of biographies, myths, folktales, and historical narratives, she addressed the power of literature to capture children's imagination. She stated, "Whether these . . . are drawn from the recent past or from some long-ago reaches of human history is not the critical factor in their accessibility to children. Rather it is the nature of the story told, its power to capture the imagination of children, to draw them into the historical event or human dilemma . . ." (p. 36). One major intent of using literature in the development of units of study focusing on history is to elicit and maintain student interest in the social studies content. To create a meaningful environment is to encourage the students to *become* participants in historic events as they become involved in the daily lives of historical figures.

Making Instruction/Assessment Connections

Under the direction of the National Council for the Social Studies, the standards for social studies education were approved in April 1994. Denny Schillings (1994), as president of the NCSS, voiced his concern that:

> No standards . . . will have much of an impact unless the teacher develops appropriate instruction for the students in his or her own classroom. Standards are, after all, to help teachers know what is important, how they can approach teaching so that students will learn those important things, and ultimately to provide guidance or specific methods to assess student progress in attaining them.

This succinctly states the concern that there needs to be an alignment between instruction and assessment. Too often a major purpose of assessment has been to assign grades. Purposeful assessment is a tool for teachers to use as they plan relevant classroom instruction. Appropriate assessment will provide teachers with immediate feedback related to individual progress to help determine what students know and what remains to be learned.

Frequently, it is not necessary or desirable to formally test students at the end of all lessons; however, an ongoing assessment plan is necessary. Effective assessment is most often integrated with instruction. Ongoing assessment provides teachers with information to determine, plan, and implement subsequent instruction.

Ongoing assessment can include, but not be limited to, teacher observations, interviews with students, student projects, student portfolios, and journals. The most effective assessment frequently includes opportunities for students to think critically in relation to the subject matter taught. Chapter 5 includes an open-ended form of assessment that illustrates a test item designed to encourage students to include content knowledge and their own thinking. The item provided is appropriate to assess student knowledge in relation to their knowledge of events leading to a conflict with Mexico. An additional assessment item has been included to assess student understanding of historical and locational skills.

Although general—rather than specific—assessment examples are indicated in most of the lesson plans, this assessment discussion concludes by stressing the importance of making assessment/instruction connections. In 1991, NCSS issued a position statement that called for *"transforming student assessment from an overreliance on machine-scored standardized tests to approaches that balance such measures with more authentic performance assessments"* (NCSS, p. 171). This is intended to reinforce the importance of making assessment/instruction connections an integral part of the social studies program.

In conclusion, it is hoped that this brief inclusion of ideas related to ongoing assessment will encourage teachers to develop strategies consistent with the standards set forth by the National Council of Teachers of Social Studies. As more and more teachers begin to make instruction/assessment connections, students will indeed be provided with a curriculum that is meaningful, integrative, value-based, challenging, and active (NCSS, 1994).

References

Crabtree, Charlotte. (1989, Winter). "History is for children." *American Educator*, 34–39.

Joyce, B., & Weil, M. (1980). *Models of Teaching* (2nd ed.). Englewood Cliffs, NJ: Prentice Hall.

National Council for the Social Studies (NCSS). (1994). *Curriculum Standards for Social Studies* (Bulletin 89). Washington, DC: Author.

Risinger, Frederick C. (1992). "Trends in K–12 social studies." Clearinghouse for Social Studies/Social Science Education, Bloomington, IN. Office of Educational Research and Improvement (ED), Washington, DC EDO-SO-92-8.

Schilling, Denny. (1994, April/May). "Teaching the human condition through the social studies." *Social Education*, *58*(4), 197-199.

Acknowledgments

I would like to thank the following reviewers of this text: James Mitchell, California State University-Dominguez Hills; and Lynn Burlbaw, Texas A&M University.

I also wish to acknowledge the contribution of my son, David Morin, for the technical assistance he provided during the writing of this book. He provided many of the computer-generated graphics as well as assistance in the preparation of the final disk copies of the manuscript and graphics.

Social Studies Instruction Incorporating the Language Arts

1 Animal Stories from around the World

GRADE ONE UNIT
Focus: Understanding Culture through Stories

LESSON TOPICS
- Two Different Ways to Look at a Familiar Story
- Stories as an Expression of Culture
- Sequencing Story Events That Depict Customs
- The Comparison of Similar Folk Tales
- Animal Stories That Explain Their Markings or Colors

Unit Rationale/Broad Goals

Unit Focus: *National Council for Social Studies Standards*

Strand 1. Social studies programs should include experiences that provide for the study of culture and cultural diversity. Young children will be provided opportunities to develop an awareness of cultural diversity through literature-based experiences (NCSS, 1994).

First-grade children are ready to develop a sense of cultural diversity and appreciation for the ways in which others express their beliefs and ideas. One way to understand and to respect cultural diversity is to explore stories told by people around the world. The ideas expressed in the stories in this unit are told through animals in ways that will captivate the imagination and interest of young children. As students read and listen to their old favorites told from the viewpoint of others, the world becomes a little smaller.

Generally, first-grade students have been exposed to traditional stories such as the *Three Little Pigs*; however, one intent of this unit is to encourage students to look at familiar stories in other ways. This early exposure to a simplified version of critical thinking is one way to encourage the students to explore and appreciate the views of others. The colorful, delightful stories are intended to serve as examples to provide teachers with a framework to extend the ideas in this unit or to select other appropriate themes.

The strategies and activities suggested in this unit focus on ideas that will guide teachers as they provide students with opportunities to enhance their learning. Suggested instruction includes student involvement in sequentially developed activities intended to develop and reinforce basic skills, as well as provide opportunities for students to participate in collaborative activities that allow for an exchange of ideas. Additionally, Bulletin 87 (1992),[1] a National Council for the Social Studies publication, is an excellent resource to provide teachers with an understanding of cooperative activities when teaching social studies. In Bulletin 87, David and Roger Johnson, Robert Slavin, and Robert Stahl address research findings and practical ideas to engage children in an interactive environment.

Provisions are made to meet a variety of student needs and to provide assistance when necessary. For example, using puppets to dramatize a story may provide a sense of security for those who are reluctant to "be on stage." The various modes of learning are included in the form of audio (reading), visual (pictures and modeling), and kinesthetic activities (making puppets). The major intent is to include experiences that provide for the study of cultural diversity through stories, as well as to reinforce basic skills through reading, writing, illustrating, and dramatizing story ideas.

Lesson 1: Two Different Ways to Look at a Familiar Story

Time Frame: 1 to 2 days

Materials/Equipment: *Three Little Pigs* (traditional); *The Three Little Wolves and the Big Bad Pig* (Trivizas), chart or mural paper, pictures that depict story characters or events, transparencies of the story frame pages, and story frame copies for each student to illustrate *The Three Little Wolves and the Big Bad Pig*.

Broad Objective: This first lesson in Animal Stories from around the World will set the stage for an understanding that similar stories may be different due to the traditions and beliefs of those telling the stories.

Specific Objective: After the teacher reviews *Three Little Pigs*, models a story frame sequence, and reads *The Three Little Wolves and Big Bad Pig*, the students will:

1. Illustrate and present a series of story frames that depict specific events in *The Three Little Wolves and the Big Bad Pig*.

Anticipatory Set (Motivation): "Most of you have heard the story about the Three Little Pigs." Show the book and elicit from the students ideas about the story and the characters. The teacher may choose to read excerpts and to pro-

---

[1]National Council for the Social Studies. (Bulletin 87, 1992). *Cooperative Learning in the Social Studies Classroom: An Invitation to Social Study*. Washington, DC: Author.

vide examples of story frames that depict major events. The story frame format is illustrated in Figure 1.1. The teacher will provide visual examples by drawing pictures and labeling events in story frames on large chart or butcher paper. The teacher could use previously prepared pictures or choose pictures from magazines. The students will be asked to indicate how the author described the wolf and the three little pigs. For example: "Do you think the wolf was considerate and wanted to help the three little pigs? Were the three little pigs able to solve their problem? How?" The teacher will continue eliciting student ideas about the story and complete the story frame chart depicting the major events. Figure 1.1 is an example of one frame in the sequentially developed story.

Input: "The story we have put in order is the usual way the Three Little Pigs story is told. However, another author had a different view of that same story. Listen carefully as I read the story titled *The Three Little Wolves and the Big Bad Pig.*" As the story is read, the teacher will emphasize story events by writing simple sentences in story frames on a large chart. The teacher will show the students the pictures that correspond with the events. After the story is completed, the teacher will tell the students they are going to complete their own picture story by creating a picture about each sentence on a story frame page.

Modeling: The teacher will give each student story frame pages. After a discussion eliciting the order of events in the story, the teacher will model the subsequent student task on an overhead transparency or on large paper. The first

The first little pig built his house out of straw.

Figure 1.1   Example of a Story Frame

frame will be modeled by the teacher. After the sentences in each frame are read, the students will be directed to illustrate the remaining sentences in each frame.

Guided Practice/Independent Practice: The teacher will circulate to provide assistance while the students complete their assignment.

Closure: The students will discuss their story frames. The teacher will guide them as they make comparisons between *The Three Little Pigs* and *The Three Little Wolves and the Big Bad Pig* stories. An emphasis will be on the difference in the actions of the story characters even though the stories are very similar. The teacher focuses on the differences that may be due to the views of the authors: "Other stories that come from faraway places may be different from those that we know best. For example, many stories are about animals; yet the people write about events and characters in a way that they understand best. Tomorrow we are going to begin reading two different stories about mice. One story we know well; however, the other story was told many years ago in China."

Lesson Extension: The teacher could ask the students to cut out the story frames they completed today. They will staple them together to form their own book about *The Three Little Wolves and the Big Bad Pig*.

Assessment: The teacher will discuss with the children and examine their story frames to determine if they have met the objective of this lesson.

The Three Little Wolves and the Big Bad Pig

(1) Story Event One

(2) Story Event Two

(3) Story Event Three

(4) Story Event Four

(5) Story Event Five

(6) Story Event Six

(7) Story Event Seven

(8) Story Event Eight

Draw your favorite part of the story.

Lesson 2: Stories as an Expression of Culture

Time Frame: 3 days

Materials/Equipment: *If You Give a Mouse a Cookie* (Numeroff), *Town Mouse, Country Mouse* (Brett), puppet example, paper plates, popsicle sticks.

Broad Objective: The students will understand that well-known stories may have different versions if told by people living in different parts of our country.

Specific Objective: After reading and comparing two mouse stories, the children will make puppets and retell the stories.

Day 1

Anticipatory Set (Motivation): "Yesterday we read about little pigs and wolves. Today we are going to read about a special mouse who liked cookies. We know most children love cookies! What would you do if I gave you a cookie?" (Of course, the children will react in the most common way: "We would eat it.") (Tape a picture of a mouse on the board.) "What do you think would happen if I gave this mouse a cookie?"

(Elicit ideas from the children. These ideas can be clustered around the book title written on the board as in Figure 1.2.) "Listen carefully as I read a story about a mouse who liked cookies and what happened when the mouse was given a cookie. We will add your ideas around the picture on the board." (Read the story *If You Give a Mouse a Cookie*. Stop at appropriate points to elicit student ideas and add them to the board.)

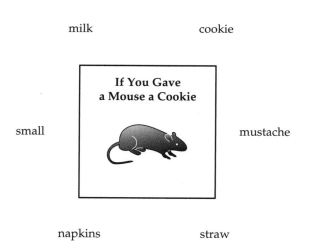

Figure 1.2   Example of a Book Cluster: *If You Gave a Mouse a Cookie*

Input: "Today we are going to begin reading different stories that tell us about mice, their thoughts, and their homes. (Show the book *Town Mouse, Country Mouse.*) This story is about one mouse family who lived in town and another mouse family who lived in the country. Before I read this story I am going to show you pictures of the mice. (The picture might be the book cover taped to the board to allow the teacher to write descriptive words under the pic-ture.) As I read the story, listen for the different events in the story and what the mice thought about the places they visited."

Closure: After the story is read, the teacher will elicit story events from the students and add their thoughts under the picture. (Example: The town mouse family decided they would go to visit the country.) "Tomorrow we are going to practice a play about this book."

Day 2

Modeling and Guided Practice: Review the story events in *Town Mouse, City Mouse.* The teacher might talk through a mouse stick puppet as the events are reviewed. See the puppet example in Figure 1.3. "We are going to act

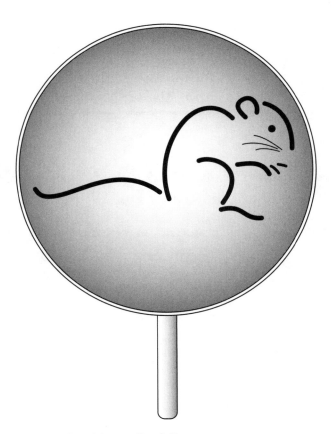

Figure 1.3   *Mouse Stick Puppet*

out the events in this story by talking through puppets that look like our story characters."

The teacher will:

1. Divide the class into groups of four children.
2. Choose and designate specific events for each group of children.
(Although several groups will be given the same event, it will be interesting to see how each event is interpreted.)
3. Discuss and decide the part each member will dramatize.
4. Model making a puppet that looks like a mouse character in the book. The puppets can be made out of paper plates and craft sticks (see Figure 1.3).

Collaborative Group Activity: (It will be helpful to elicit upper grade students or parent volunteers to facilitate this activity.) The students will make their puppets. When they complete the puppets, they can practice retelling the story events through their puppets.

Day 3

As lesson closure, the students will dramatize the story. The student-made puppets could be displayed in the classroom. The teacher will evaluate student progress and success by observing the relationship between the stories and the dramatization of the stories they developed. The students will be told they will read a story the next day about another mouse who lived far away.

Lesson 3: Sequencing Story Events That Depict Customs

Time Frame: 2 to 3 days

Materials/Equipment: *The Mouse Bride* (Chang), butcher paper, chart paper, story-step example.

Broad Objective: To sequence story events reflecting customs of rural China.

Specific Objective: After reading the story *The Mouse Bride* and developing a story step map, the students will create a series of mural frames on butcher paper to depict each story step (event) in sequential order. The story frames will be created by using a comic book format in which the sentence describing the event is written inside the "cloud" as part of the mural.

Day 1

Anticipatory Set/Motivation: "The mice we read about in the past few days might have been those that lived in our immediate area. However, stories have been written about mice that live in faraway places. The story we will read about today tells us about a girl mouse who lives in China." (Find China on a world map.)

Input: As *The Mouse Bride* is read, the teacher will write events on a large chart paper in "story step" format (Figure 1.4). The teacher will pause frequently to show the beautiful pictures that illustrate each event.

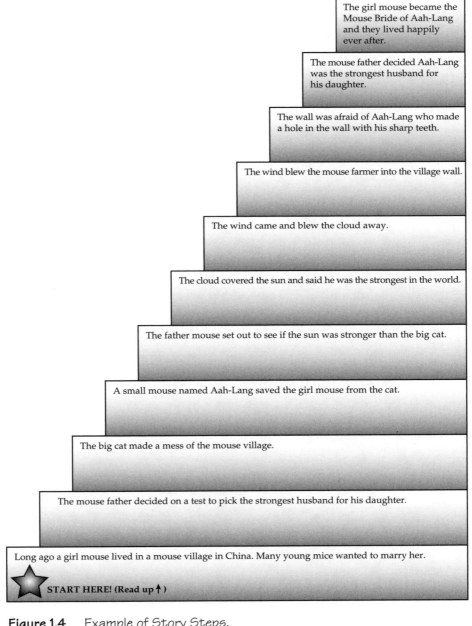

The girl mouse became the Mouse Bride of Aah-Lang and they lived happily ever after.

The mouse father decided Aah-Lang was the strongest husband for his daughter.

The wall was afraid of Aah-Lang who made a hole in the wall with his sharp teeth.

The wind blew the mouse farmer into the village wall.

The wind came and blew the cloud away.

The cloud covered the sun and said he was the strongest in the world.

The father mouse set out to see if the sun was stronger than the big cat.

A small mouse named Aah-Lang saved the girl mouse from the cat.

The big cat made a mess of the mouse village.

The mouse father decided on a test to pick the strongest husband for his daughter.

Long ago a girl mouse lived in a mouse village in China. Many young mice wanted to marry her.

START HERE! (Read up ↑)

Figure 1.4   Example of Story Steps.

 Start reading at the bottom step.

Model/Guided Practice: The teacher will review the story events by eliciting ideas from the students. After a general review of the story steps, the teacher will model one example that includes a picture and descriptive sentence taken from the story steps. Student input will be elicited as the picture is created. "What kind of picture might best illustrate this part of the story? Can you describe this picture in a sentence?" Model the procedure used in comic books that place what is said or the picture description in a "cloud."

An example of one story event is shown in Figure 1.5.

Closure: Review story events. Explain the students will create collaborative mural pictures the next day.

Day 2

Lesson Procedure (Collaborative Group Activity): Review the previously developed story "steps" (events). The class will be divided into small groups of three. Each small group of students will be provided one copy of the story steps. One step will be highlighted for each group to indicate this is the story event they will illustrate and caption. Explain the tasks.

Each student will be assigned a specific task and encouraged to provide input and help the other group members complete his or her specific story step. It is helpful to elicit cross-age tutors or parent volunteers when implementing collaborative activities with primary children.

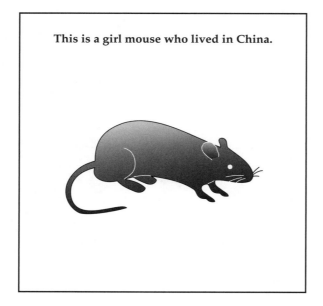

Figure 1.5 Example Story Event

Day 3
Each group will display its picture and retell the story in sequence. The teacher will review each group's story result to determine if the sequence is accurate.

Closure: The teacher will remind the students that some of the story traditions may be similar or different in the United States. The teacher should also remind the students that although the story is about mice, the writers of stories are real people who write about traditions and beliefs in the part of the world they know best. In this story, the father mouse searched in many different places to find the strongest husband for his daughter—only to find him in his own village.

Lesson 4: The Comparison of Similar Folk Tales

Time Frame: 1 to 2 days

Materials/Equipment: *The Mouse Bride* (Chang), *The Mouse Bride* (Dupre), a comparison paper, comparison paper transparency, overhead projector.

Broad Objective: The children will compare two similar folk tales that were told by people from countries that are far away from each other.

Specific Objective: After reviewing the previously read Chinese folk tale (*The Mouse Bride*) and reading the Mayan version of *The Mouse Bride*, the students will:

  1. Make comparisons by drawing and indicating events in the two folk tales.

Anticipatory Set/Motivation: The teacher will write the title—*The Mouse Bride* (A Mayan Folk Tale)—on the board and display the book. "We recently read another story with the same name. (Elicit from the children the title of the Chinese folk tale—*The Mouse Bride*.) Do you think this story is the same? What happened in the Chinese folk tale with the same name?" Remind the students that the father mouse searched for the strongest husband for his daughter.

Input: "Now we are going to hear about a different Mouse Bride. This family—like the Chinese family—is searching for the perfect husband for their daughter." (Read *The Mouse Bride, A Mayan Folk Tale*.)
  "This story takes place in the rainforest of Chiapas, a state in Mexico. (Find this area on a large map.) Listen carefully to see if the stories are the same." To focus the students on the story, stop at appropriate places to elicit ideas and add their comments under the *Mayan Mouse Bride* to make comparisons to the *Chinese Mouse Bride* story.

Model/Guided Practice/Independent Activity: After the story is read, the teacher will elicit a discussion to guide the students in making comparison between the two Mouse Bride stories. A transparency will be used to guide the students as they begin the comparison activity. The teacher will check for understanding and provide assistance as the comparison page is completed. Pictures can be drawn or cut out of magazines to be included in the space provided.

Closure: The students will be encouraged to share comparisons between the folk tales. They will be told that stories such as these may be similar; however, the focus of the story may be different. For example, the mouse family in the Chinese Mouse Bride story searched many places to find the strongest husband for their daughter, only to find him in their own village. The mouse family in the Mayan Mouse Bride story also searched for a perfect husband for their daughter. However, an additional purpose of this story is to help children understand and respect nature.

Lesson Extension: An art activity could appropriately follow this lesson. Because both stories end with a wedding celebration, the focus could be on making decorations for a celebration. Colorful tissue paper flowers can be made quite easily under the guidance of the teacher.

Comparison Activity

The Chinese Mouse Bride	*The Mayan Mouse Bride*
the big cat yes no	the big cat yes no
the moon yes no	the moon yes no
the cloud yes no	the cloud yes no
the wind yes no	the wind yes no
the wall yes no	the wall yes no
a wedding yes no	a wedding yes no

Lesson 5: Animal Stories That Explain Their Markings or Colors

Time Frame: 2 to 3 days

Materials/Equipment: *How the Leopard Got His Spots* (Kipling), "How the Chipmunk Got His Stripes" (*Crocodile! Crocodile!*, Baumgartner), chipmunk-shaped cover and chipmunk-shaped story transparencies, various animal story shapes and covers.

Broad Objective: The students will understand that some stories tell about animals and how they adapt to their environment.

Specific Objective: After the children hear stories about how animals got their specific markings, small groups of children will:

1. Collaboratively choose one animal and make decisions relating to how that animal got its color or markings.
2. Make an animal-shaped book about that selected animal.

Day 1

Anticipatory Set/Motivation: Show pictures of how animals adapt to fit into a specific environment. Examples could be the changing of fur color to reflect seasonal change (rabbits) or the chameleon that is able to change skin color rapidly. It would be particularly motivating to bring a chameleon to allow the students to observe the changes. "Many people tell stories about why animals are like they are or how they acquired specific markings. Today we will read about how some people believe two animals got their markings."

Input: "This first story is about a leopard who lives in a forested part of Africa (show the country on a map). The spots on the leopard are very helpful because the color and markings protect him. This book tells about how one writer thought the leopard got his spots." Read the story *How the Leopard Got His Spots*. During the reading write important ideas on the board.

Modeling/Guided Practice: "Today we are going to write a short class story about another animal that had a special marking. This story takes place in the United States. It has been handed down for generations by Native Americans in an attempt to tell how the chipmunk got his stripes. Listen for the information because we are going to write a story about the chipmunk."

After reading the story, the teacher will elicit ideas and guide the students in forming at least one to three sentences about how the chipmunk got his stripes. The teacher will model this by writing the story on large lined chart paper in the shape of a chipmunk. The children will be guided through proofreading the story and making any necessary changes. The students will be told that they are going to write animal stories the next day and place them in animal-shaped books (show a transparency of the chipmunk book cover).

Day 2

Collaborative Group Activity: (This activity works most efficiently if older students or parent volunteers are available to help the teacher monitor the small group activities.) In preparation for this part of the lesson, the teacher will have copied the story the children wrote about the chipmunk on smaller lined paper cut in the shape of a chipmunk (Figure 1.6). A cover/back page was made for the story by cutting heavy paper in the shape of a chipmunk (Figure 1.7). Details to emphasize the chipmunk's features and the title were added to the front cover. The story is stapled inside the cover and the back page.

After the animal-shaped story is discussed, the students are told they will develop their own animal books in small groups. The teacher provides the following directions:

1. The children will work in groups of three to begin developing an animal story.
2. The first task for Day 2 is to select an animal they wish to write about. Each group will select one animal. The following list will be provided as examples of animals they might choose (lion, bobcat, leopard, giraffe, panda, polar bear, dog, cat, horse, or one that is not listed).
3. Several animal books from the school library will be available for the students to browse through for ideas.
4. Each student is responsible for writing at least one sentence.
5. The teacher will bring Day 2 activities to a close by telling the students to look for any pictures they might want to add to their story.

Figure 1.6   Animal Story Example

Day 3

1. The teacher will review the task and regroup the students.
2. Each group will be provided the appropriate animal-shaped lined paper, cover, and back.
3. The students in each group will be given a number from 1 to 3. The number they were given will determine their task in the group. For example: All members of the group will add ideas or suggest changes for the story.

The student given number 1 will rewrite the story on the animal-shaped paper.

The student given number 2 will cut out and add details to the cover.

The student given number 3 will cut out the animal shape for the back page and search for appropriate pictures in magazines that can be added to the story or the cover.

Closure: The teacher will observe student accuracy and understanding of the markings of the chosen animals as each group of students has the opportunity to present their story to the class. Each story will be highlighted by being placed around a picture of a large world map or globe centered on a bulletin board or a wall. This display will be captioned *Stories from around the World*. It will be an excellent culmination for this unit of study. An example of this display appears in Figure 1.8 (p. 16).

Figure 1.7   Example of Back Cover

Animal Stories from around the World

Figure 1.8   Animal Stories from around the World

One Direct Instruction Format Example

Topic/Subject _____   Grade Level _____

Materials/Equipment:

Broad Objective:

Specific Objective: [often called a Behavioral Objective or an Instructional Objective] State specifically (1) *What task the learner will do*, (2) *under what conditions*, and (3) *at what level of performance* (if appropriate).

Motivation: [often called *Anticipatory Set*] Focus the students on what they will learn. This may be in the form of reviewing past learning. Objects, pictures, or stories can be used to stimulate interest.

Objective and Its Purpose: Let the students know the intent of the objective and the purpose of the subsequent activity.

Input: Provide the necessary information. Develop the skill in a sequential manner.

Model: [Related to and can be combined with the input activity] Model and provide examples using the equipment or materials the students will use later. An example or two should be developed and illustrated on the board, an overhead projector, or a chart. Involve the students in this process.

Check for Understanding: Check by asking questions during the lesson. Ask the students to provide a rationale for their answers.

Guided Practice: Allow the students to practice tasks similar to those they will do independently. The teacher is present to provide assistance/feedback.

Independent Practice: Provide appropriate independent practice to reinforce the skill objective. The teacher does not necessarily provide assistance.

Closure/Evidence of Mastery: Indicate method you will use to determine student understanding or mastery of the specific objective.

Provide for Differences: Use audio, visual, or tactile materials appropriate for the learners. Provide appropriate reinforcement or challenge activities. Centers could be utilized for such activities.

Related Literature

Baumgartner, Barbara. (1994). *Crocodile! Crocodile! Stories Told Around the World*. New York: Dorling Kindersley.

Brett, Jan. (1994). *Town Mouse, Country Mouse*. New York: G.P. Putnam's Sons.

Chang, Monica. (1992). *The Mouse Bride*. Flagstaff, AZ: Northland Publishing Co.

Dupre, Judith. (1993). *The Mouse Bride*. New York: Alfred A Knopf.

Gleeson, Brian. (1992). *Anansi*. Saxonville, MA: Picture Book Studio.

Johnson, Tony. (1995). *The Iguana Brothers*. New York: Scholastic.

Kipling, Rudyard. (Illustrated by Lori Lohstoeter) (1989). *How The Leopard Got His Spots*. Saxonville, MA: Picture Book Studio.

National Council for Social Studies. (Bulletin 87, 1992). *Cooperative Learning in the Social Studies Classroom: An Invitation to Social Studies*. Washington, DC: Author.

National Council for Social Studies. (Bulletin 89, 1994). *National Standards for the Social Studies* (pp. 21–30). Washington, DC: Author.

Numeroff, Laura. (1985). *If You Give a Mouse a Cookie*. New York: Harper-Collins Publisher.

Trivizas, Eugene. (1993). *The Three Little Wolves and the Big Bad Pig*. New York: Simon & Schuster's Children Publishing Division.

2 Families and Their Traditions

GRADE TWO UNIT
Focus: People Who Make a Difference

LESSON TOPICS
- People Who Are Important to Me
- Families Are Unique
- Special Happenings I Remember
- Family Traditions
- Special Ways to Carry on Traditions
- Preparation for a Multicultural Celebration of Traditions

Unit Rationale/Broad Goals

Unit Focus: *National Council for Social Studies Standards*

Strand 2. Social studies programs should include experiences that provide for the study of the ways human beings view themselves in and over time.

Strand 4. Social studies programs should include experiences for children that provide for the study of individual development and identity and the people who made a difference in their lives (NCSS, 1994).

The primary purpose of this unit of study, *Families and Their Traditions*, is to provide second-grade students with meaningful, integrated experiences that enhance their instruction and learning. It includes the use of literature as a vehicle to elicit interest, reinforces basic reading and writing skills, and focuses on experiences that provide for the study of individual development and identity. Related literature will be an integral part of instruction throughout this unit as the students study the ways human beings view themselves in and over time.

The integration of listening, reading, writing, and basic language skills will be reinforced utilizing suggested social science content. An emphasis will be on the development of students' social participation skills as well as on the acquisition of basic information to facilitate student understanding of others.

Learning experiences will be provided that encourage active student involvement. The students will be encouraged to cooperate and share in many activities to actively engage them in their learning. The students will have opportunities to use their dramatic and artistic abilities as they share their efforts with others when they plan and implement a multicultural celebration of traditions.

Although this unit focuses on examples of selected cultures and traditions, the ideas are presented to serve as a catalyst for teachers. The omission of specific cultures/traditions was not meant to diminish others and their beliefs. The ideas presented are intended to be examples that will encourage teachers to include family traditions of equal importance and interest.

Overall Evaluation

The unit lessons are designed to encourage ongoing assessment in which instruction and assessment are integrated. Student progress and needs will be determined by using a combination of evaluative and assessment tools. The lesson activities allow for assessment that provides the students with immediate feedback. This approach to assessment could include observation charts, student folders, written student reactions, student projects, and student presentations.

Lesson 1: People Who Are Important to Me

Time Frame: 1 to 3 days

Materials/Equipment: *All Kinds of Families* (Simon), apple paper, "Class Apple Tree," overhead projector, apple transparency, crayons, markers, pencils.

Broad Objective: The students will become aware of the different people who help them.

Specific Objective: Students will describe and write stories on apple-shaped paper about someone important to them or how that person helped in some way. The apple stories—with their pictures—will be added to the "Class Apple Tree" bulletin board.

Day 1

Anticipatory Set: The teacher will elicit a discussion about many different kinds of families. Student discussion will lead into reading the story, *All Kinds of Families*. "Today we will read about the differences in families—just as your own family may be different from other families you know."

Input: Read and show illustrations in *All Kinds of Families*. During the reading, focus on differences in families, yet emphasize that families and other people—who are like family members—are important to us. After reading the story, the teacher can focus on how other people are important to us. For example, our class members are important to us. We help each other when we work and play together. We are with one another a great deal of the time, we work and play together, and at times need to solve problems together. "Each person in this class is a valued member in this room. Today we will begin to grow our own class tree to show that we are all important to one another."

Model: Focus on a large apple tree attached to a bulletin board or wall that will soon be filled with "apples" created by the students. (The apple tree can be constructed by using green and brown butcher paper, tissue paper, or construction paper.) A transparency made from the apple example (shown in Figure 2.1) can be projected on a screen by using an overhead projector. This will provide students with ideas and an example of the apples that will be attached to the tree. The apple "story" could include a name, description of student, and anything special the student wishes to share. The students could be encouraged to finish the sentence—"One person who helps me is . . ." A teacher-constructed apple— including a picture—will serve as an example and encouragement for others to complete their "apples" for the "Class Apple Tree" (Figure 2.2 on p. 22).

Guided/Independent Practice: The teacher will circulate to provide assistance as the students write their rough drafts. As the students finish writing their ideas, they will be encouraged to edit the rough draft, then copy it on the final "apple" paper.

Day 2

Closure: This project may be completed on day 2. Remind the students to bring the photograph they wish to add to their apple story. Explain the "Letter to Parents" the students will take home today. This letter includes information about the upcoming unit. It will be helpful to include a list of items, such as a photograph, that the students will need to complete this unit.

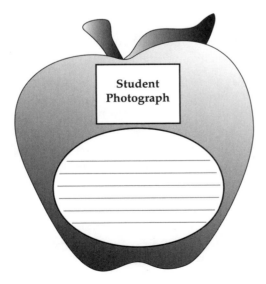

Figure 2.1   *Example Apple for Class Tree*

OUR CLASS APPLE TREE

Helping Each Other in Work and Play

Figure 2.2 Bulletin Board Example: Class Apple Tree

Day 3
The completed apple stories and pictures can be shared. After students share their efforts, the apples can be attached to the "Class Apple Tree" bulletin board.

Assessment: Because the objective of this lesson is to build student awareness of the different people who are important to them, the assessment will be informal and ongoing. Throughout this unit the teacher will continue to assess student needs informally and providing an observation chart or teacher notes will be a helpful reminder of student needs when planning subsequent activities.

Lesson 2: Families Are Unique

Time Frame: 1 to 3 days

Materials/Equipment: *A Chair for My Mother* (Williams), *All the Colors of the Race* (Adoff), poetry paper, acrostic poem examples.

Broad Objective: Students will develop descriptive language as they build an awareness that family members who provide care may be different, yet the needs may be similar.

Specific Objective: After discussing families and reading related literature, the students will write and illustrate acrostic poetry about their families.

Day 1

Anticipatory Set: The teacher may begin this lesson with a short discussion about different kinds of families. "Yesterday, we discussed families as people who help one another and work together—such as the people in our class. However, we usually think of a family as being people to which we are related, such as our parents, grandparents, sisters, and brothers. Each of our families is special to us, yet families may be different. Today we will read about ways in which families might be different."

Input: *A Chair for My Mother* can be read to illustrate one family (a mother, daughter, and a grandmother). After reading, the discussion may focus on the specific family in the story. The student reactions can be clustered on the board to provide examples of descriptive language. This will be helpful when the students write their poems.
    Example:

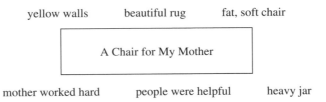

The students should be encouraged to choose their own descriptive words when they write their poem about special families. They can be told the family they choose to write about may be their own or an imaginary family. The students will be reminded that the descriptive words will be helpful when they draw a picture of their "family" poem. Their illustrated poems will become part of a class poetry book.

Modeling: The poem "All Colors of the Race" will be read as an example of a special kind of family. The teacher will explain a simple acrostic poem and model examples of variations (see examples).

Father's name is Harry	Fun
Anna is my mother	And
Many children	Merry
In many states	Interesting
Lively	Likes to read
Yet loving	Yours may be different

Guided Practice: During this time each student will write his or her own acrostic poem. By creating poetry about their families, the children will be enhancing writing skills by developing poetry that is meaningful. Before the students begin writing, the teacher may elicit ideas from the children to help them verbalize their ideas for their own acrostic poems. This will help the teacher check for understanding and reinforce the task expectations. The students will be encouraged to write a rough draft, then the teacher will provide each student with a form on which they can rewrite their poetry and draw a family picture (see Figure 2.3). Continuous guidance and feedback should be provided by the teacher.

Closure: As the students may not complete this task in one lesson, the teacher can stop at this point to review student progress and the tasks that remain before the project is complete. Students should be encouraged to do their best work because the acrostic poetry and pictures will become a class book.

Day 2

Independent Practice: The students will be assigned the task of completing this project as homework. This is an opportunity for other family members to become part of this project. The next day, the children will have an opportunity to share their finished poetry before it becomes part of the class book of poems. The book should be laminated because it will be read over and over by the students.

Figure 2.3   Family Picture/Poem Pattern

Lesson 3: Special Happenings I Remember

Time Frame: 2 to 3 days

Materials/Equipment: *Where the River Begins* (Locker), *The Patchwork Quilt* (Flournoy), quilt squares (fabric or construction paper), overhead projector, quilt transparency, markers, example patchwork quilt (if possible).

Broad Objective: The children will share and illustrate family experiences.

Specific Objective: After reading relevant literature and discussion students will:

1. Describe and illustrate on quilt squares experiences they shared with family or others.
2. Combine the squares to form a class quilt.

Day 1

Anticipatory Set: The teacher will show pictures and discuss people working, playing, and sharing special experiences. Students will be encouraged to share some special experiences before the teacher reads *Where the River Begins*. This book illustrates two boys sharing a camping trip with their grandfather.

Input: "The story we just read is an example of one special experience the two boys shared with their grandfather. These events were remembered for a long time. Today we are going to read about a lady who had a special way to remember important events that happened in her family." Before reading *The Patchwork Quilt*, the students should be encouraged to listen for the important events and how the grandmother made sure they were remembered. During reading, focus on how the patchwork quilt told a story by representing a special family event or experience on each square. After the reading of *The Patchwork Quilt*, elicit a discussion about the experiences represented by each square. The children will be told they will have the opportunity to illustrate their experiences.

Input/Modeling: If possible, the teacher should share a real patchwork quilt. If not, a colored picture of a patchwork quilt will serve to reinforce the various designs and colors that are often part of a quilt. "Today we are going to begin our own patchwork quilt that illustrates an experience or event for each person in this class." Using an overhead projector (or large chart paper), the teacher will model an example quilt square. The example square illustrates a birthday, holiday, or a special event that is memorable. The teacher will demonstrate the combining of the squares to form one large quilt on a wall. The squares could be constructed out of fabric or construction paper. The students will be encouraged to be creative in their designs.

Independent Activity: The students will begin their rough drafts as the teacher facilitates to assure student success.

Closure: The students will be reminded they will complete their quilt squares the next day. They will be encouraged to get input from their families.

Subsequent Days: Students will have the opportunity to finish their quilt squares. Time will be provided for each student to share his or her square before it becomes part of the class patchwork quilt. Those who finish early could be encouraged to write a story describing the illustrated experience.

Lesson 4: Family Traditions

Time Frame: 2 to 3 days

Grouping: Whole class; groups of 2 to 3 if desired.

Material/Equipment: *Lion Dancer* (Waters & Slovenz-Low), *Tet: The New Year* (Kim-Lan Tran), boxes for dioramas, magazines for collages, origami or folding paper, *Origami, Indian Lore* (Thorneycroft).

Broad Objective: The children will gain an understanding for the traditions of others.

Specific Objective: After reading relevant literature and guided practice, the students will illustrate and describe a family tradition or a tradition they choose to illustrate.

Day 1

Anticipatory Set: The teacher will tell the students that many families celebrate special events by following long established practices, or traditions. These traditions can be described as the handing down of stories, beliefs, and customs from generation to generation. After discussion, student ideas will be elicited and clustered on the board around the word *tradition*.

Cluster Example:

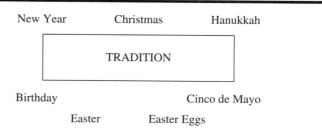

Input: "Today we will learn about other traditions that are important to new arrivals to the United States, such as the Vietnamese. We will also learn about traditions that have been with us for a longer period of time as we read about events that occur during Chinese New Year and the artistic images created by Native Americans. We will begin with the story *Tet: The New Year.* This story provides us with information about a most important holiday in Vietnamese communities." As the story is read, the teacher will add special facts to the "tradition" cluster on the board (such as rice cakes, dragon dance, firecrackers).

Another tradition can be illustrated by reading the story *Lion Dancer.* This story depicts a young Chinese boy and his family as they prepare for the Chinese New Year celebration. The focus can be on the meaning for this celebration, food preparation, practicing the dance, and the Chinese lunar calendar (see examples in the book). The ideas will be reinforced by adding them to the cluster on the board.

"A third way many people carry on customs and traditions is through their art. One example is a special way of creating images by folding paper—a Japanese art form called origami. Some Native American people also developed a form of art by folding paper to represent animals or birds in their stories."

Modeling/Guided Practice: The students can be actively involved in the process of paper folding. Excerpts from *Origami, Indian Lore* can be read to provide examples of folding paper that illustrate stories passed from generation to generation. Provide students with the appropriate paper, then model and guide them as they create a simple design such as a teepee or a thunderbird. (See the examples provided in the *Origami, Indian Lore* book.)

Closure: The students will share their models. They will be asked to come the next day with ideas about a family tradition they wish to illustrate. The teacher will provide some example/ideas about ways in which their ideas might be illustrated (dioramas, paper folding, collages, etc.). The students could use their own family traditions, or they might wish to depict a tradition of others. The teacher should review some of the traditions previously discussed. The students will be encouraged to bring pictures from magazines, old greeting cards, or other materials that will be useful if they wish to develop dioramas or collages. The teacher might also choose to allow small groups of children to work together on a project.

Days 2 and 3:   The tradition projects will be completed. The students should be encouraged to write descriptions to accompany their projects. The students will share and display their "traditions." They will be encouraged to compare their traditions with those of other class members to illustrate their understanding of the traditions of others.

Lesson 5: Special Ways to Carry on Traditions

Time Frame: 2 to 3 days

Grouping: Groups of 3 to 4

Materials/Equipment: *The Remembering Box* (Clifford), *Cherokee Summer* (Hoyt-Goldsmith), mural paper.

Broad Objective: Students will develop an understanding that traditions are carried on in many ways.

Specific Objective: After reading relevant literature, the students will develop a mural that depicts ways to carry on traditions.

Day 1

Anticipatory Set: "Our past readings and activities have provided many ideas about our traditions as well as the traditions of others. Today we will read about special ways people have carried on their traditions/customs. Later we are going to make a large class mural that illustrates and describes many traditions."

Input: "Often people keep items that have a special meaning. We call these items artifacts or treasures, or just hand-me-downs. *The Remembering Box* is a book that tells how these items reveal the history of one family. Listen carefully because we are going to list the items and discuss the special story they told." After reading excerpts, elicit a discussion about how some families remember events by saving artifacts. These ideas may clustered on a chart, the board, or on an overhead projector.

The Remembering Box is an excellent book to read to the students. This book tells the story of a grandmother sharing family traditions with her young grandson. As the grandmother shares her "remembering box," these ideas can be added to the cluster developed during the reading of *The Remembering Box*.

"The families that we read about today had a special way to remember and carry on their traditions by saving family treasures and artifacts. Others carry on their traditions by demonstrating crafts and skills learned from past centuries. One example is revealed in the book *Cherokee Summer*. This book is about a Cherokee girl, Bridget, whose family carries on its traditions by demonstrating skills and crafts." As the book is read, the students will become aware of the Cherokee Heritage Center in Tahlequah, Oklahoma, the history of the Cherokee tribe, and the skills and traditions they passed on to their children. The book focuses on the food, songs, and the stomp dance that have been passed on for centuries. The pictures provide excellent visuals to help the students understand the demonstration of traditions and customs.

Modeling/Guided Practice: The teacher will provide an example of a mural idea that demonstrates how one might illustrate/describe or caption a specific tradition. One example might be an illustration of a dragon and the Chinese New Year as shown in Figure 2.4. The students will be organized into groups of 3 or 4. Each group will decide on a specific tradition to illustrate and describe. Resources might include books and magazines to provide ideas. If time allows, the students will begin the rough draft. The teacher should remind the students of specific traditions they have read about, such as New Year, Christmas, Easter, birthdays, Hanukkah, or some other family tradition.

Closure: The students will be told they will continue this project during the next day or two. Their independent task will include the gathering of ideas they will add to their group effort. In subsequent days the students will continue their rough drafts. The teacher will provide directions for the development of the final mural. The butcher paper will be marked off to indicate boundaries for each group to depict its tradition. Separate panels might be cut for easier handling. The required markers, paints, and pencils will be available, and time frames for the actual work will be allotted. Weather permitting, the mural paper and materials might be organized outside.

Each group will be encouraged to write captions or describe its section of the mural.

Figure 2.4   Example Section for the Class Mural

Lesson 6: Preparation for a Multicultural Celebration of Traditions

Time Frame: 2 to 3 days

Materials/Equipment: *Three Stalks of Corn* (Politi), *Globalchild—Multicultural Resources for Young Children* (Cech).

Broad Objective: Students will begin preparations for the multicultural celebration of traditions.

Specific Objective: The students will culminate this unit of study by celebrating understanding and respect for the traditions of others.

Day 1

Anticipatory Set: The teacher will elicit a general discussion about the previous activities in this unit of study. "There are many ways to celebrate the exciting traditions we have been learning about during the past few weeks. One way is to demonstrate the skills and ideas we have learned and to have fun while doing so. Let me read about one way to celebrate traditions and customs."

Input: The teacher will read *Three Stalks of Corn*. During the reading the teacher will focus on the traditions that are based on necessity—the use of the corn plant. This story includes legends, food, and the doll making that have been passed on from one generation to the next. These traditions were shared in a special celebration—the fiesta. "We, too, can have a special celebration to enjoy many of the traditions we have read about. During the next few days we will prepare for our celebration—Our Multicultural Celebration of Traditions!"

The teacher and the children will discuss the preparation for their celebration. The teacher will elicit ideas concerning activities and entertainment they might want to include. Based on the following list of plans for this special event, the teacher and the students will determine the responsibilities for the preparation and the actual Multicultural Celebration of Traditions. The students will need several days to practice the presentations they will participate in on the special day.

Preparation Plans for the Multicultural Celebration

First: Get Permission from the Principal to Hold This Celebration!

1. Select a repertoire of multicultural skits, songs, dances, poetry, etc. (The Cech book is an excellent resource.)
2. Determine participants for each presentation/activity.
3. Determine costumes or appropriate clothing to be worn for each activity.
4. Practice the skits, songs, and dances.

5. Develop a program of activities.

6. Plan the food menu.

7. Elicit parents/volunteers to bring food, plates, and other needs.

8. Elicit parents with special skills or talents to participate.

9. Plan for environment:
- Seating arrangement
- Decorations
- Display areas for art and crafts and other student projects developed during the course of this unit
- Food booths or tables
- Presentation area (stage)
- Dance/music area

10. Send out invitations.

11. Additional needs will surface as you prepare.

12. The unit culmination—the Multicultural Celebration of Traditions. Have fun!

Related Literature

Adoff, Arnold. (1982). *All the Colors of the Race*. New York: William Morrow & Co.

Adoff, Arnold. (1973). *Black Is Brown Is Tan*. New York: Harper-Collins Publishers.

Cech, Maureen. (1991). *Globalchild—Multicultural Resources for Young Children*. New York: Addison-Wesley.

Chalking, Miriam. (1990). *Hanukkah*. New York: Holiday House.

Clifford, Eth. (1985). *The Remembering Box*. Boston: Houghton Mifflin Company.

Flournoy, Valerie. (1985). *The Patchwork Quilt*. New York: Dial Books for Young Readers.

Hoyt-Goldsmith, Diane. (1993). *Cherokee Summer*. New York: Holiday House.

Locker, Thomas. (1984). *Where the River Begins*. New York: Penquin Books.

National Council for Social Studies. (Bulletin 89, 1994). *Curriculum Standards for the Social Studies* (pp. 21–30). Washington, DC: Author.

Politi, Leo. (1993). *Three Stalks of Corn*. New York: Charles Scribner's Sons.

Simon, Norma. (1976). *All Kinds of Families*. Niles, IL: Albert Whitman & Company.

Spann, Mary Beth. (1991). *Literature-Based Seasonal and Holiday Activities*. New York: Scholastic.

Tran, Kim-Lan. (1992). *Tet: The New Year*. New York: Simon & Schuster.

Thorneycroft, Edward. (1992). *Origami, Indian Lore*. New York: Mallard Press.

Waters, Kate, & Slovenz-Low, Madeline. (1990). *Lion Dancer*. New York: Scholastic Inc.

Williams, Vera B. (1982). *A Chair for My Mother*. New York: Mulberry Books.

3 Communities

GRADE THREE UNIT

Focus: Their Differences and Needs

LESSON TOPICS

- What Is a Community?
- People Gather from Many Places to Form Communities
- All Communities Have Basic Needs
- Community Helpers
- Community Involvement

Unit Rationale/Broad Goals

Unit Focus: *National Council for Social Studies Standards*

Strand 3. Social studies programs should include experiences that provide for the study of people, places, and environments.

Strand 5. Social studies programs should include experiences that provide for the study of interactions among individuals, groups, and institutions.

Strand 7. Social studies programs should include how people organize for the production, distribution, and consumption of goods and services (NCSS, 1994).

The primary purpose of this unit of study, *Communities: Their Differences and Needs*, is to provide third-grade students with meaningful, integrated experiences that help them understand how people create places that reflect ideas, personality, culture, and basic needs. It includes the use of literature as a vehicle to elicit interest and focus on the concept that communities have differences and similarities. Related literature will be an integral part of instruction throughout this unit as the students begin to think about continuity and change in their own locality.

Strategies

One overall strategy is to build bridges between other subject areas. The integration of listening, reading, writing, and basic language skills will be reinforced utilizing suggested social science content. An emphasis will be on the development of students' social participation skills as well as on the acquisition of basic social studies knowledge and skills.

Examples of teaching models utilized in this unit are indicated below:

A. The Reception/Oriented Concept Attainment Model

The Concept Attainment Model of teaching was designed to develop inductive reasoning, concept development, and analysis (Joyce & Weil, 1980). Although there are several variations of the Concept Attainment Model, the reception model was selected to develop Lesson 3—All Communities Have Basic Needs. The Reception/Oriented Concept Attainment Model—developed from the work of Jerome Bruner, Jacqueline Goodnow, and George Austin—is implemented in teacher-directed phases. The phases are generally presented in the following sequence:

(1) Presentation of Data and Identification of concept

(2) Testing Attainment of the Concept

(3) Analysis of Thinking Strategy

A detailed description of the Concept Attainment Model can be examined in *Models of Teaching* (Joyce & Weil, 1980).

B. Collaborative Activities: A Group Investigation Model

The mission or goal of the group investigation model is the "development of skills for participation in democratic social process through combined emphasis on interpersonal (group) skills and academic inquiry skills" (Joyce & Weil, 1980, p. 12). An example of the group investigation model can be examined in Lesson 4—Community Service: Community Helper. This format was adapted from the work of Herbert Thelen and is implemented in phases that allow students to explore a situation, event, or problem by formulating study groups in which they carry out designated assignments.

After appropriate research, each group presents its data and progress of its investigation. As they analyze, the students may discover a new concern as a result of their investigation. In this case, they would recycle and investigate the new situation or problem (Joyce & Weil, 1980).

There is a great deal of literature focusing on various forms, implementation, and effectiveness of cooperative learning; however, much of the recent work has been conducted by Robert Slavin at the Center for Research at Johns Hopkins University. The following resources provide detailed information related to cooperative activities:

Slavin, Robert. (1990). *Cooperative learning, theory, research, and practice*. Englewood Cliffs, NJ: Prentice Hall.

Kagan, Spencer. (1989). *Cooperative learning*. Riverside: University of California.

Learning experiences will be provided that elicit student interest and involvement. The students will be encouraged to cooperate as they participate in many experiences intended to actively engage them in their learning. The students will have opportunities to use their dramatic and artistic abilities as they share their efforts with others.

Although this unit focuses on a limited number of community examples, the ideas are presented to serve as a catalyst for teachers when they develop units that reflect specific localities and the way in which they evolved over time. This specific unit focuses on the gathering together of people and the subsequent formation of groups responsible for providing services and basic needs. A community provides much more than basic needs. The bonding of people living together in communities often results in providing support to those in need. The ideas presented are intended to be examples that will encourage teachers to focus on specific localities, people, needs, and unique characteristics.

Overall Evaluation

Because the major focus of this unit is on building an awareness of diverse communities and their needs, the lessons are designed to encourage ongoing assessment in which instruction and assessment are integrated. Student progress and needs will be determined by using a combination of evaluative and assessment tools. The lesson activities allow for assessment that provides the students with immediate feedback. This eclectic approach to assessment could include observation charts, student folders, written student reactions, student projects, and student presentations.

Lesson 1: What Is a Community?

Time Frame: 2 to 3 days

Materials/Equipment: *Going to Town* (Wilder), *Little House in the Big Woods* (Wilder); large outline map of the immediate community, cutout examples representing the school, library, hospital, stores, parks; pictures of different kinds of communities (city, farm, small town); markers, crayons, paper and pencil, paint, scissors, Venn diagram example.

Broad Objective: Students will understand that communities are places where groups of people settle. Communities are alike because they are places were people know one another and often work and play together. Communities may be different due to location, organization of buildings, geography, size, and the time frame in which they were developed.

Specific Objective: After reading stories and exploring different kinds of community pictures the students will:

1. Create a Venn diagram illustrating the differences and similarities of two communities.
2. Illustrate/label their homes, and identify stores, schools, parks, libraries, hospitals on a large bulletin board map outline.

Figure 3.3 Model for Store

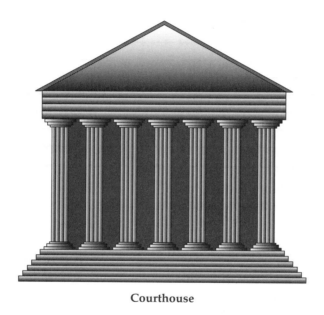

Courthouse

Figure 3.4 Model for Courthouse

Extended Activity: A diorama example illustrating a community will be discussed. A diorama is a miniature three-dimensional model depicting a selected scene. The scene can represent a specific community scene such as a park, shopping center, a home appropriate for that particular climate and geography, or an immediate part of the community well known to the students. The identifying features and the materials used to develop the diorama will be explained. Shoe boxes, small cardboard boxes, milk cartons (small and large), tongue depressors, twigs, sand, or other materials can be brought from home by students who have designed a specific diorama they choose to develop. The students will write stories about their projects. These projects will be shared and displayed in the classroom.

Figure 3.5   Example of a Seashore Diorama

The diorama in Figure 3.5 is an example of a seashore scene. It can be constructed by lining the bottom and sides of a shoe box with the desired shades of tissue, crepe, or construction paper. The beach umbrella is a miniature model; however, a student may choose to add houses or other models.

Lesson 2: People Gather from Many Places to Form Communities

Time Frame: 1 to 2 days

Materials/Equipment: *How My Family Learned to Eat* (Freidman), *Stringbean's Trip to the Shining Sea* (Williams), postcards, postcard transparency, large U.S. map.

Broad Objective: Students will develop an understanding of the diverse geographic origins of people who live in communities.

Specific Objective: After reading related literature, the students will:

1. Trace the travels of people on a large world map as they move from one community to another.
2. Write postcards about specific locations or geographic areas.

Anticipatory Set: Focus the students on a large world map centered on a bulletin board. Elicit a discussion about the many parts of the world from which people come. Point out geographic points of interest. Read the story *How My Family Learned to Eat*. Emphasize the distances they traveled and the ways they might have kept in touch with family members. "Today we are going to read about a journey that took one person through different areas of the United States."

Input/Modeling: Elicit a discussion about *Stringbean's Trip to the Shining Sea.* Focus on the way in which Stringbean let other family members know about special events and places during his journey. Read the book, stopping at pertinent sections to emphasize the use of postcards that illustrate specific landmarks. After reading the story, the teacher can share a postcard that illustrates a landmark from a specific geographic area or community (town or city) known by class members. Since many students have moved from one community to another, they will be asked to develop postcards to illustrate those communities and/or other familiar landmarks.

Closure: The teacher might bring closure to Day 1 of this lesson by asking the children to think about a community they were once part of or one they visited. The students will be asked to bring this information the next day, or they can bring information about a community they would like to visit. This information will be used as they develop postcards.

Day 2

Input/Modeling/Guided Practice: The teacher will share information and a postcard about a move from one community to another. This will be followed by discussing the movement of people from one community to another.

The discussion includes input about the use of postcards to tell others about places of interest they visited during their move. A transparency of a postcard that illustrates a well-known place of interest will be projected (see Figure 3.6). The teacher will elicit information and model the written message and the address to be added to the postcard. The message should include information about the picture on the postcard. The students will be told that this postcard and those they develop will become part of a bulletin board.

Independent Activity: Students will each be given a postcard-shaped paper. They will design a picture, decide to whom they will send this postcard, and write the address and message on their postcard. The children will have the

Figure 3.6   Postcard Example

option of illustrating a specific community, a place they visited, or a place they would like to visit.

Closure: The students will share their postcards, point out on a large map placed in the center of a bulletin board the geographic location of each specific postcard. The cards will be clustered around the map. Colored yarn can be used to direct connect each card to the appropriate map location (see Figure 3.7).

Lesson Extension: A research center supplied with maps, books, and task ideas can be developed to encourage the students to read about other geographic areas. Example: One task could be a story starter such as: "If I lived or visited (_____), I would see . . .". This will reinforce creative writing skills as well as map and research skills.

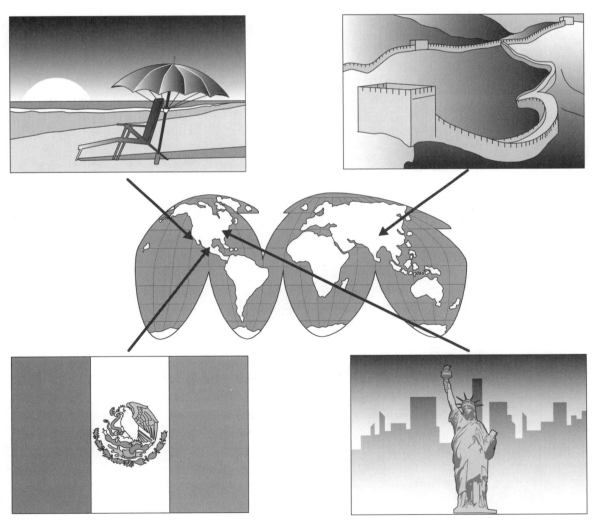

Figure 3.7   Map/Card Example

Lesson 3: All Communities Have Basic Needs

Time Frame: 3 to 4 days

Materials/Equipment: *House of Snow, Skin and Bones* (Shemie), *Mound of Earth and Shell* (Shemie), *Houses of Wood* (Shemie), *A Fruit and Vegetable Man* (Schotter), picture set describing and illustrating several communities, word list of selected items, individual student chart format, magazines, glue, scissors, poster board.

Broad Objective: Students will recognize that communities may be different; however, they all have basic needs (food, clothing, shelter).

Specific Objective: After reading about the basic needs in selected communities, the students will:

1. Listen to information, form concepts, and make judgments regarding that information.
2. Develop a chart illustrating the basic needs of selected communities.
3. Develop collages indicating specific basic needs and how they are acquired.

Day 1

Anticipatory Set: The teacher will read excerpts from selected stories and elicit a discussion to review communities explored in earlier lessons. These communities will be located on a large map. The communities discussed should be selected to include differences in climate, size, and geography. The teacher will tell the students they are going to play a game about with how communities might be alike.

Lesson Procedure: (This lesson will be implemented in phases associated with a Reception/Oriented Concept Attainment model of teaching).

Phase One: Presentation of Data and Identification of Concept

1. *The teacher will present labeled examples.* The following words will be written on the board in a prearranged order and labeled *yes* or *no*.

video game (no)	bread (yes)	coat (yes)
skates (no)	house (yes)	milk (yes)
bicycle (no)	television (no)	vegetables (yes)
toys (no)	apartment (yes)	radio (no)
shoes (yes)	doll (no)	baseball mitt (no)

The students are told there is one idea that all the *yes* examples have in common. "I have an idea in my mind related to all the items labeled *yes*."

2. *The students are asked to compare and justify attributes of the positive and negative examples.* The teacher will ask the students to think about what the words labeled *yes* have in common and record these responses on the board. (Example: Some people live in houses and some people live in apartments.)

3. *The students are prompted to generate ideas and test hypotheses.* The teacher will elicit responses by asking the students to think about what the idea may be. What attributes lead them to that idea? The students will be asked why their choices are possible. If a student indicates he or she knows the idea, the teacher will ask that student to hold that thought until most of the students seem to have an idea about the concept. When most of the students seem to know the idea, they will be asked to share them. The teacher will write the generated ideas on the board.

4. *The students state a definition according to the essential attributes.* They will be asked to state the rule of the concept according to its attributes. What attributes helped define their concept? (Example: "I think the idea is all people need food because all the food words are labeled *yes*.) The hypothesis is not confirmed until the next phase.

Phase Two: Testing Attainment of the Concept

1. *The students will be asked to identify additional unlabeled examples as* yes *or* no. The teacher tells the students they will test to see if their ideas are correct. The teacher writes additional examples on the board. The students are asked to label them *yes* or *no* based on their ideas.

VCR _____   camera _____   pants/shirt _____
jacket _____   fish/meat _____   houses _____
microwave oven _____ baseball bat _____   fruit _____

After eliciting responses about the unlabeled samples, the teacher will confirm the hypothesis. The students will be told the *yeses* are basic needs of communities. The teacher will continue to state that although communities may be different, all communities need food, clothing, and shelter.

2. *Students will generate examples.* The teacher will test further by asking the students to generate additional examples to be labeled by the other class members. The student generating each example will verify if it was labeled correctly.

Phase Three: Analysis of Thinking Strategy

The teacher will question the students and guide them as they describe their thought patterns to determine the secret idea. Some may have organized their thoughts into broad categories and then narrowed them to specifics. Did they group all the food first or did they focus on the labels? The teacher will ask students what attributes they focused on and why. They will be asked if they focused on one attribute at a time or did or did they focus on several initially and arrive at their idea through elimination? The students will be asked what process they followed if the hypothesis they chose was not confirmed. Did they continue to use their previous strategy or was the strategy changed to develop a new hypothesis?

Closure: The teacher will review and chart information related to communities and their specific basic needs. This information will come from stories that had been read earlier as well as from the textbook. Each student will be provided a Basic Needs chart (see Figure 3.8) to complete as the teacher guides this procedure on an overhead projector. As the teacher elicits past learning from the students, they will be reminded the charted information will be helpful the subsequent day.

Day 2

Before the independent practice is assigned, the teacher will review the Basic Needs chart completed the previous day. Students will be reminded that communities have similar basic needs; however, the specific nature of those needs and the way they are acquired may be different due to size, climate, and geography. During this activity the students will:

1. Work together in groups of three.
2. Be provided magazines, scissors, heavy poster board, and glue.
3. Choose one community and illustrate its basic needs by making a collage of pictures and words cut out from the magazines.

Community	*Food*	*Clothing*	*Shelter*

Figure 3.8   Basic Needs Chart

Day 3

The students will:

1. Complete the collage.
2. Write a summary explaining their communities, their specific basic needs, and how they acquired these basic needs.

Day 4

The students will share the collages and summaries with the entire class. The collages will be displayed on classroom wall.

Lesson 4: Community Helpers

Time Frame: 3 to 4 days

Materials/Equipment: *My Mother the Mail Carrier* (Maury), *The Library* (Stewart), *Firehouse* (Winkleman), butcher paper, markers, pencils, crayons, paint and brushes, magazines, scissors, paste, boxes, and dowels.

Broad Objective: The students will recognize that communities require specific services that are provided by community members or helpers.

Specific Objective: After reading books and exploring community helper charts, the students will:

1. Complete in each group a mural that depicts and captions one community helper providing a service for their community.
2. Report and summarize the data to determine community helper needs.

Anticipatory Set: "Let's pretend we are going to start a new community. We know we will need food, shelter, and clothing from our past discussion about basic needs of all people. (Refer to the illustrations completed in a prior lesson.) In our community we are going to need special people who can do specific jobs to help and protect us. Sometimes these people provide services—such as the librarian, firefighter, or the mail carrier." List the book titles on the board and elicit services each community helper provides. Pause at appropriate places to elicit input from the students and add to each list.

Lesson Procedure: (This lesson will be implemented using a Group Investigation Model.)

Phase One: Encounter a Puzzling Situation
"In the book I just read, we have seen how the mail carrier is an important part of a community." (Elicit a short discussion about the services provided by the

mail carrier. Add the student responses to the board list.) "Do you think we will need mail service if we start a new community?" After discussion, pose questions that encourage student thinking. Example: "Do you think we need other helpers to provide services for the community we are planning?"

Phase Two: Explore Reactions to the Situation
The above question prompts the students to react. The teacher guides the students by questioning them about their own needs and experiences. Examples: "Who do you visit for health examinations? Have your ever had a fire in your home or nearby? Who helped your family put the fire out?" As the students react, the teacher will draw attention to the specific needs they expressed and point out those who provided help. They will be guided into noticing the number of helpers they will need to provide services as they plan for their community needs.

Phase Three: Formulate Study Tasks and Study; Organize for Study
As the students become aware of the various services provided by community helpers, the teacher will guide them in structuring the task by outlining the helpers and the duties that will be required. The teacher will tell the students that he or she has a list of people who function as community helpers. "Each of the following people work in his or her own special way to help." List the following people on the board and display community helper pictures (firefighters, doctors, nurses, teachers, police officers, mail carriers). "We are going to find out how these workers provide services for our community. What kind of questions will we need to answer?" The teacher will guide the students in forming a list of questions such as:

- What is the title of this specific community helper?
- When do we need the help of this person?
- Where does this helper provide his or her service?
- What tools or knowledge does this worker need to provide help?
- How does this person provide help?

The students are given the task of making murals depicting community helpers. The teacher will tell the students they will be divided into study groups. Each group will illustrate one community helper providing a service for the community. The illustrations will be captioned and/or labeled. See examples in Figure 3.9.

The students may draw their own pictures or they may cut out pictures from magazines. (The roll of butcher paper will be precut to assure the size will be appropriate for a subsequent lesson utilizing this mural as story rolls.) The students will be reminded to use the above questions as a guide to choose pictures and to illustrate appropriately.

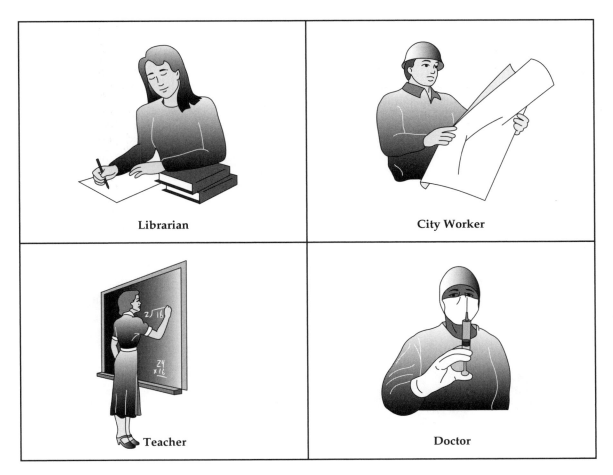

Figure 3.9   Community Helper Mural Examples

The teacher will find it helpful to group the students according to interest in the specific community helper. After the study groups are formed, the students will select a community helper to illustrate, choose a group member to be the recorder, one to read the questions, and one to be the spokesperson.

Phase Four: Independent and Group Study
Each group will carry out its assignments. The students will be guided into reviewing the list of questions to remind them as they make decisions about how they will depict their community helper on the mural. Work on the mural will begin; however, this lesson activity will require two to three days. The groups will be encouraged to continue gathering materials at home each evening for the next day. The next day the students will continue developing their mural. When they have completed the mural, the group will summarize the work for the spokesperson.

Phase Five: Analyze Progress and Process

The small groups will report back to the class to talk about the progress they have made on their project. Each group will present its pictorial data (mural/caption/labels) and analyze its progress. Groups will also report on the process. (How did group members reach their goal?) The teacher will guide them in evaluating the pictorial data in an attempt to help the students determine if they met their objective. ["What kind of community helpers might we need to provide services in a newly planned community?"]

Phase Six: Recycle Activity

(Closure and motivation for a subsequent lesson.) The students may have discovered a new problem as a result of discussion in this group activity. In that case, the group may wish to recycle and investigate a new situation. "What do people do in small communities if they do not have a regular fire department?" After discussion, pose questions that encourage student thinking. Example: "Do you think we need other helpers to provide services for the community we are planning?"

Extended Activities

1. The students can create story roll boxes. Each group will dramatize its own rolled-up mural. The story box can be made by cutting off the top flaps of a cardboard carton so the front of the box looks like a television screen when it is placed with the open side facing the audience. Each group can roll its story on two dowels with the picture side exposed. Attach the top dowel in the holes near the top of the box and place the bottom dowel in the two holes cut out near the bottom of the box. The first frame of each story will fill the open front side of the box. Make certain the dowels extend outside the box to allow for easier turning as the story pictures are revealed. Each group will have the opportunity to provide a "movie" for the other class members. Remember, the spokesperson is the narrator and will tell the story as the story is unrolled.

2. The students could visit a local community service such as the fire station or a hospital.

3. A community helper could be invited to speak to the class.

Lesson 5: Community Involvement

Time Frame: 2 to 3 weeks, including the project

Materials/Equipment: *Tikvah Means Hope* (Polacco), *Sing to the Stars* (Barrett), *Everglades: Buffalo Tiger and the River of Grass* (Lourie), *Save the Earth* (Miles), trash collection charts, trash bags and cans.

Broad Objective: Students will recognize that community members work in different ways to support one another and to improve their community.

Specific Objective: After reading stories about specific contributions to selected communities, the students will:

1. Become actively involved to improve their community by planning and implementing a recycling project.

Anticipatory Set: "During this unit of study you have became aware of the meaning of 'community,' as well as differences, similarities, and how basic needs are provided in most communities. However, another important need must also be discussed. That is the basic need for community members to support one another in their daily lives as well as in times of need. I have two special stories that describe events in which community members supported those in need." (Display *Sing to the Stars* and *Tikvah Means Hope*.)

Input/Modeling: The teacher will focus the students by eliciting and clustering ideas around book titles written on the board as key ideas are read. Examples are illustrated below:

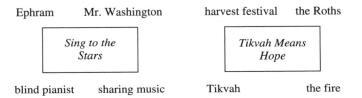

After the books are read, the teacher will elicit more ideas and add to the book title clusters on the board. This will lead into a discussion related to the kind of support and activities that people can be involved in to improve their community. The teacher may choose to illustrate present day environmental concerns through the eyes of a concerned citizen. *Everglades: Buffalo Tiger and the River of Grass* (Lourie) is an excellent book that delivers an important message through the eyes of a Native American chief, Buffalo Tiger. After excerpts from the book are read, the teacher can guide the students in brainstorming the kinds of projects in which they can participate to better their communities.

Guided Practice: The students will be encouraged to think locally as they examine possible projects. The teacher can list several kinds of projects to explore. The book *Save the Earth* (Miles) is an excellent resource to guide this initial search for a project. The following ideas can be listed on the board and discussed to help the students choose their project.

1. Search in your neighborhood and school for all the ways in which energy is wasted. This should encourage student research to discover alternate energy sources. As a class, make a list of alternate choices and write letters to the town council to suggest ways to lessen this waste.

2. What can be done to reduce food waste? The students might do a research project focusing on their own school cafeteria. Collect data and chart it to determine the amount of food waste. Develop a plan to lessen this waste. Present your ideas to the school administrators and the cafeteria staff.

3. Research and prepare a fact sheet on plastic containers. Send a group to a local fast-food restaurant and ask the manager about plans for reducing the use of plastic. Be prepared to present suggestions. Investigate and chart the amount of trash your school accumulates each day. How can your class improve this situation? Guide the students in selecting a project and planning the steps to complete their project.

Trash Collection, Recycling Project

The following steps are included as one example project:

1. Brainstorm your ideas as a class.
2. Make an outline of the project objective and procedure.
3. Write a preliminary project plan and get it approved by the principal.
4. Break your class into groups that will be responsible for different categories of trash (glass, plastic, paper).
5. Chart the usual amount of trash collected in each category (weight or volume; check with the custodians). See example chart in Figure 3.10.
6. Plan for specific ways, containers, and locations to collect the trash.
7. Make calls to determine where the recycling centers are located in your community.

TRASH COLLECTION CHART			
	Amount collected	**Trash container**	**Other places trash was found**
Trash			
Plastic			
Glass			

Figure 3.10   Trash Collection Chart

8. Arrange for volunteers (parents) to transport the trash to the recycling center.
9. Regroup as a whole class to determine how the recycling process can continue on a regular basis at your school. This leads into a second project. Suggest a realistic procedure and reasons for continuing this project to the principal.

Follow-up Activity:

1. Determine as a class how you can spend the money you made by recycling trash to benefit the community.
2. One suggestion: The class might buy a tree and/or plants to beautify the school grounds or another area in the community.

Related Literature

Barrett, Mary Brigid. (1994). *Sing to the Stars*. New York: Little, Brown and Company.

Freidman, Ina R. (1984). *How My Parents Learned to Eat*. Boston: Houghton Mifflin.

Joyce, B., & Weil, M. (1980). *Models of Teaching*. Englewood Cliffs, NJ: Prentice Hall.

Lourie, Peter. (1994). *Everglades: Buffalo Tiger and the River of Grass*. Honesdale, PA: Boyds Mills Press.

Maury, Inez. (1991). *My Mother the Mail Carrier*. New York: Feminist Press.

Miles, Betty. (1991). *Save the Earth*. New York: Alfred A. Knopf.

National Council for Social Studies. (Bulletin 89, 1994). *National Standards for the Social Studies*, (pp. 21–30) Washington, DC: Author.

Polacco, Patricia. (1994). *Tikvah Means Hope*. New York: Bantam Doubleday Dell Publishing Group.

Sandin, Joan. (1981). *A Long Way to a New Land*. New York: Harper & Row.

Schotter, Roni. (1993). *A Fruit and Vegetable Man*. Boston: Little, Brown and Company.

Shemie, Bonnie. (1989). *Houses of Snow, Skin, and Bones*. New York: Tundra Books.

Shemie, Bonnie. (1989). *Mounds of Earth and Shell*. New York: Tundra Books.

Shemie, Bonnie. (1989). *Houses of Wood*. New York: Tundra Books.

Stewart, Sarah. (1995). *The Library*. New York: Farrar/Straus/Giroux.

Wilder, Laura Ingalls. (1995). *Going to Town* (adapted from *Little House in the Big Woods*). New York: HarperCollins Publishers.

Williams, Vera B. (1988). *Stringbean's Trip to the Shining Sea*. New York: Scholastic.

Winkleman, Katherine. (1994). *Firehouse*. New York: Walker and Company.

4 California after 1848: A Period of Rapid Growth

GRADE FOUR UNIT

Focus: Events That Linked California to the Rest of the United States

LESSON TOPICS
- The Discovery of Gold in California
- Gold Rush Topics
- The Pony Express
- The Transcontinental Railroad
- A Timeline of Events That Indicate Rapid Growth in California

Unit Rationale/Broad Goals

Unit Focus: *National Council for Social Studies Standards*

Strand 1. Social studies programs should include experiences that provide for the study of culture and cultural diversity.

Strand 3. Social studies programs should include experiences that provide for the study of people, places, and environments.

Strand 5. Social studies programs should provide for the study of interactions among individuals, groups, and institutions (NCSS, 1994).

Fourth-grade students are ready to extend the study of their immediate region and explore the history of the state in which they live. The history of each state has unique events that contributed to the way in which it grew and changed. This unit is an example that illustrates the rapid change and growth that occurred in California following the discovery of gold. This unit will provide teachers throughout the United States with suggestions to focus students on events that reflect specific characteristics of their own states.

Several events occurred after 1848 that changed the face of California forever. The discovery of gold and the completion of the transcontinental railroad resulted in rapid growth as California became linked to the rest of the United States. In an effort to bring California history and geography to life for the students, stories have been selected that focus on major events and the people who participated in this period of rapid growth.

Stories about the people that populated California will allow the students to understand their diversity and respect their contributions. The selection of a small number of events is intended to provide an in-depth study into one period of rapid growth. This focus will set the stage for future units of study that makes links to growth patterns.

The lesson plans include independent as well as collaborative activities to meet the various student needs and differences. The students will explore the geography of the United States as well as California when they focus on the various modes of travel chosen to reach California. Research, writing, and art activities will provide meaning and reinforce basic skills. The students will develop a time line to illustrate and put in perspective the period in which these major events occurred. Instruction and assessment connections will be ongoing to provide students with immediate feedback, to plan subsequent lessons, and to enhance student understanding of the events and people that accelerated the rapid growth in California.

Lesson 1: The Discovery of Gold in California

Time Frame: 3 to 4 days

Materials/Equipment: White and blue butcher paper, markers, wall maps (North America, South America, United States, California), a large outline map of North and South America, California outline map, map transparencies, individual maps for each student, *The Historical Albums of California* (Wills), *The World Rushed In* (Holliday), *The Pioneers Go West* (Stewart), *By the Great Horn Spoon* (Fleischman), miniature ship example, overhead projector.

Broad Objective: The students will explore geography in relation to the discovery of gold in California.

Specific Objective: After viewing a video and reading literature, the students will begin a large class story map and individual maps that illustrate the geography of the United States, California, and the ways in which people came to California.

Day 1

Anticipatory Set/Motivation: "In the 1840s people began to move westward to settle in parts of California. (Locate California on a large wall map and discuss California in relation to the rest of the United States. This will be followed by focusing the students on an outline map of California on an overhead projector, Figure 4.1.) During this time, Mexico, who controlled California, began to give large land grants to encourage settlement. As a result, John Sutter

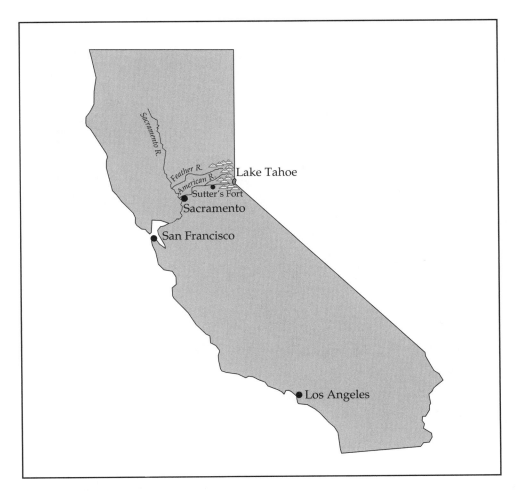

Figure 4.1   Map of California

received a large land grant and developed a fort on the Sacramento River. (Point out these areas on the transparency during this discussion.) Slowly people began to settle in California; however, in 1848 an event occurred that changed California forever. Today we will read about events that triggered rapid growth in California. Listen carefully to the events that increased the population from about 12,000 to 250,000 people between 1848 and 1852. Be ready to discuss where the people came from and how they got to California."

Input/Modeling: Read excerpts from *The Historical Albums of California* (Wills), pages 21, 26–29. Review the area in which gold was discovered in relationship to the rest of the United States (see Figure 4.2 on p. 56). This will be followed by a discussion focusing on how the people came to California.

Prior to this lesson center a large outline map that includes South America as well as North America on a bulletin board covered with blue butcher paper (see Figure 4.3 on p. 57). The outline map can be enlarged by using an overhead

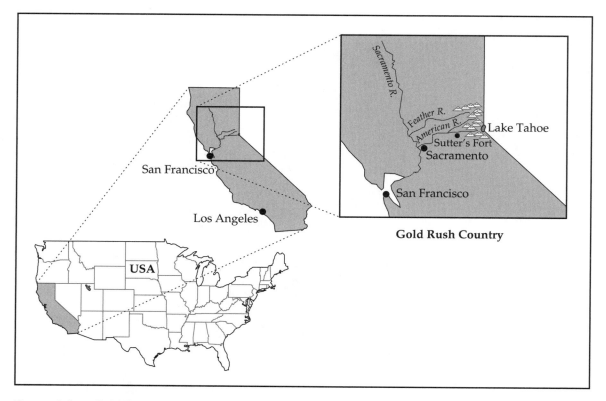

Figure 4.2   *Gold Rush Country*

projector to project a large image on white butcher paper. That image can be outlined with a marker. This map will grow as the story of the movement into California unfolds. Guide the students as they indicate the following major routes to California:

1. Traveling overland in wagons
2. Traveling by ship around the tip of South America or by way of the Isthmus of Panama.

Closure: Following a review of the major routes, the closing focus will be on the overland route taken by most immigrants. Excerpts from *The Pioneers Go West* will be read to illustrate the experiences of those traveling in wagon trains. The frequently used overland routes will be indicated on the bulletin board map after key excerpts have been read.

Day 2

Modeling/Guided/Independent Practice: Following a review of the major routes taken to California, excerpts from *The Pioneers Go West* will be read to illustrate traveling overland in a covered wagon. Each student will be provided an individual outline map of the United States (see Figure 4.4 on p. 58 and Fig-

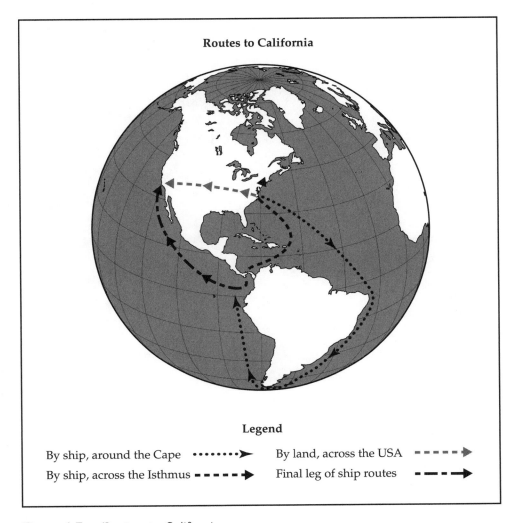

Routes to California

Legend

By ship, around the Cape   • • • • • • • • ➤   By land, across the USA   – – – – – ➤

By ship, across the Isthmus ■ – ■ – ■ ➤   Final leg of ship routes   ■ – ■ – ➤

Figure 4.3   Routes to California

ure 4.5 on p. 59). The teacher will use a transparency made from this map to guide the students as they draw in dominant land forms and frequently used overland routes.

Closure: The teacher will elicit ideas related to other ways people traveled to California. After reading accounts from *By the Great Horn Spoon*, the teacher will tell the students they will hear more about the adventures of Praiseworthy and Jack as they continue their journey to California.

Days 3 and 4

The book *By the Great Horn Spoon* will be read by the students to integrate reading instruction and enhance social studies instruction. While the students are reading this book, they will write brief summaries of specific events that

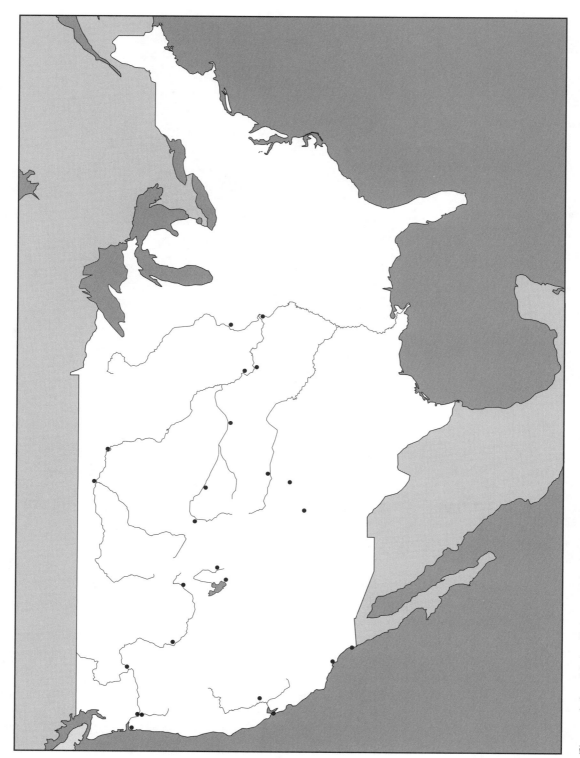

Figure 4.4 Major Points in Westward Movement

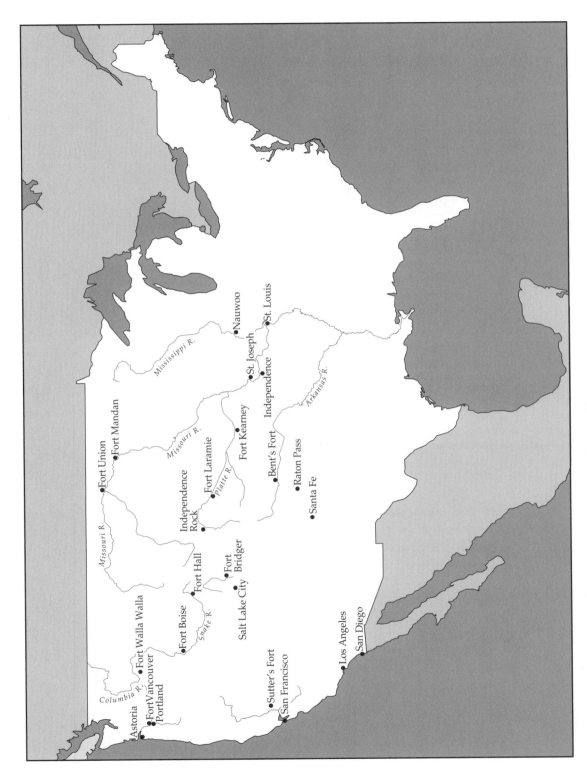

Figure 4.5   *Major Geographical Locations during Westward Movement*

Praiseworthy and Jack Flagg set out on a ship bound
from Boston to the California gold fields in 1849

Figure 4.6   Events in Journey to the Gold Fields

occurred as Praiseworthy and Jack journeyed to California. The teacher will model writing a summarized event beneath a miniature ship cutout (see Figure 4.6). The stories will be shared and placed in strategic locations around a large world map on a bulletin board.

Lesson 2: Gold Rush Topics

Time frame: 2 to 4 days

Materials/Equipment: *Dame Shirley and the Gold Rush* (Rawls), *Chang's Paper Pony* (Coerr), *By the Great Horn Spoon* (Fleichman), *The Gold Rush Era* (Quontamatteo and others), maps, accounts of the gold discovery, mural paper, charts, markers.

Broad Objective: The students will work collaboratively to research and illustrate designated gold rush topics.

Specific Objective: After reading relevant literature, the students will:

1. Outline information about the discovery of gold in California.
2. Develop mural sections that depict selected aspects of the gold rush.

Day 1

Anticipatory Set/Motivation: "Our previously read stories focused on the large numbers of people who quickly populated California and the way in which they traveled to reach the gold fields. People from all walks of life caught the 'gold fever.' The Forty-Niners came from all areas of the United States, chose different routes to California, and had a variety of experiences. (Review routes on the map.) Today we are going to learn more about the life in boom-towns and in the diggings."

Input/Modeling/Guided Practice: Read excerpts from *Dame Shirley and the Gold Rush*, *Chang's Paper Pony*, and *By the Great Horn Spoon* to provide eye-witness accounts and factual information. The headings indicated below will be written on the board or charted to focus the students on these main topics. During the readings, the teacher will elicit student input and model the outlining of pertinent information related to major gold rush topics. Example supporting ideas will be indicated under the appropriate topic.

1. People who came to California
2. Why people came to California
3. Routes to California
4. Life in California boom towns
5. Life in the diggings

Closure: The students will be told they are going to work in small groups as they illustrate and summarize in writing a mural section. The class will be divided into five groups. Each group will be given one of the topics listed above. Relevant literature will be discussed and made available to allow the students to read more about their topics. A resource library of related historical fiction and factual books will provide students with the additional information they can add to the existing outline. Additional readings and research for information to complete their outlines may take several days. The outlines will provide ideas as the students develop the murals and write summaries.

Days 2 and 3

Group Activity: The teacher will review group tasks and elicit progress reports from each group. The students will be provided a list of geographic and political features. (Examples are the routes, mountains, Sacramento, Sutter's Fort, Sacramento and American Rivers.) They will add these to their personal maps and to murals, if appropriate. Each group will continue its tasks and prepare for a presentation to the entire class.

Day 4

Each group will present its mural section to the entire class. All sections of the mural will be displayed in the classroom along with a written summary of the applicable specific topic.

Lesson Extension

1. The students could participate in a simulation of life and adventure in a frontier mining camp. (Resource: *Gold Rush. Interact: Learning Through Involvement*, 1-800-359-0961.)

Lesson 3: The Pony Express

Time Frame: 2 to 3 days

Materials/Equipment: *The Record Ride of the Pony Express* (video), VCR, "The Pony Express: 1860–1861" (*Cobblestone: The History Magazine*), *Buffalo Bill and the Pony Express* (Coerr).

Broad Objective: The students will become aware of efforts to link California with the rest of the United States.

Specific Objective: After viewing a video and reading stories about the Pony Express, the students will:

1. Trace the route of the Pony Express riders on the large bulletin board map and on individual United States outline maps.
2. Write letters from California to family or friends in eastern United States.

Day 1

Anticipatory Set/Motivation: "When we read about the adventures of Praise-worthy and Jack Flagg we learned about the lack of communication they had with Aunt Arabella back in Boston. A letter took months to go from California to Boston. The mail was carried overland in wagons or stage coaches and by ship around the tip of South America or by way of the Isthmus of Panama. The need for faster communication between east and west heightened when California was admitted to statehood in 1850. The video we are going to watch examines one system that hastened the delivery of mail for a brief period of time."

Input: "Watch carefully to learn about the Pony Express system that flourished for a brief period in 1860. Take notes related to the usual route taken, the miles that were traveled in a short period of time, and the problems the riders had as they attempted to deliver mail quickly. Later you will indicate the route on a map and write letters that will be delivered by Pony Express."

Show the video *The Record Ride of the Pony Express*. After the video, the teacher will elicit a discussion about the events and the route taken by the Pony Express riders. This route will be traced on the bulletin board map.

Guided Practice/Modeling: After a discussion about the video and the stories, the teacher will indicate on the bulletin board map the route taken by Pony Express riders from St. Joseph, Missouri, to Sacramento, California. The mail made the rest of the journey by steamship to San Francisco. The students will draw this Pony Express route on individual United States maps. The teacher will guide this procedure on a transparency made from an outline map of the United States.

Days 2 and 3

Input/Guided/Independent Practice: To make a bridge from the prior lesson and to focus on specific events, the teacher will read excerpts from *Buffalo Bill and the Pony Express* and "The Pony Express: 1860–1861". These books will become part of the class library to encourage additional reading.

The students will write letters about their experiences as though they had lived during this time. The students might actually mail the letters to another fourth grade class in other parts of the United States. The student task will be to:

1. Write a letter to a friend or family member back east.
2. Take on the character of a person who lived during this period of time.
3. Write a letter that tells about experiences in California.
4. Proofread for errors, rewrite, and address the letter.

Closure: The teacher will elicit volunteers to read the letters. One student letter or one written by the teacher might be used to model proofreading before the letter is written in a final form. The students will share their letters the next day.

Lesson 4: The Transcontinental Railroad

Time Frame: 2 to 3 days

Materials/Equipment: *The Iron Horse* (Wormser), "The First Transcontinental Railroad, 1869" (*Cobblestone: The History Magazine*), *Charlie Brown's America* (video), VCR.

Broad Objective: The students will understand the importance of the railroad in linking the East and the West.

Specific Objective: After viewing a video and reading stories about the transcontinental railroad, the students will create cartoons illustrating and charting the progress of the Union Pacific and the Central Pacific in laying the track to link the East and the West.

Day 1

Anticipatory Set/Motivation: A bridge will be made from the previous lesson that focuses on the brief success of the Pony Express. An additional focus will be on the subsequent telegraph lines and their failure to make a real link between California and the East. The need remained to find a way to lessen the long, hard journey to California usually made by wagon or by ship. It was the proposal of the transcontinental railroad that finally linked California with the rest of the United States.

Input: Stories about the first transcontinental railroad (*The Iron Horse* and "The First Transcontinental Railroad: 1869") will be read to provide background related to the events that were part of the process of laying track to link the East and the West. The teacher will show the video *Charlie Brown's America* to illustrate another way in which the story of the transcontinental railroad can be told. As the students view the video, they will be asked to look for factual information as well as the form in which the story is told.

Modeling/Guided Practice: After the video, the teacher will elicit video events from the students and cluster those ideas around the title. Example:

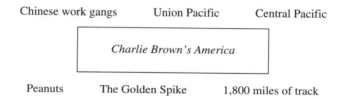

Chinese work gangs   Union Pacific   Central Pacific

Charlie Brown's America

Peanuts   The Golden Spike   1,800 miles of track

   The teacher will discuss the format of the video and tell the students they are going to illustrate the story of the transcontinental railroad using the cartoon format. The teacher will guide and elicit input from the students to make a list of additional events that will provide ideas for their cartoon stories. One frame will be modeled as an example.

> The first transcontinental railroad linked California with the rest of the United States.

Days 2 and 3

Independent Practice: The list of story ideas and the cartoon format will be reviewed. Students will create their cartoons. Relevant literature and the list of events that occurred during the building of the transcontinental railroad will be available to provide students with ideas for their illustrated stories.

Closure: The students will share their cartoon stories. The stories can be compiled into a class book to be read by the students independently or in groups. The students will be told they will begin a collaborative activity the next day that illustrates major events in the period of rapid growth in California.

Lesson 5: Time Line of Events That Indicate Rapid Growth in California

Time Frame: 4 to 5 days

Materials/Equipment: Boxes, materials for dioramas, library of relevant books.

Broad Objective: The students will illustrate visually and in written form the major events that occurred during one period of rapid growth in California.

Specific Objective: After a general review of the past lessons focusing on rapid growth in California, each small group of students will:

1. Create a diorama that illustrates an event that occurred during the period of rapid growth in California.
2. Write a summary describing the event and its effect.

Anticipatory Set/Motivation: Review and chart the past events related to the rapid growth in California. Display all the relevant books, pictures, past student work, and one example diorama. A diorama can be described as a miniature scene, wholly or partially three-dimensional, depicting figures in a naturalistic setting. Objects are often placed in a shoebox or a larger cardboard box that is open on one side to reveal the scene. The inside of the box can be painted to represent a background. Handmade or natural items can be placed inside to depict the desired scene. A diorama example is illustrated in Figure 4.7 (p. 66).

Day 1

Lesson Procedure: During this lesson the students will function in collaborative groups. The teacher will:

1. Divide the class into small groups of four.
2. Explain and provide specific tasks and instructions for each group member.
3. Provide a model diorama and summary of an example event.
4. Facilitate an initial group meeting to guide students as they make decisions related to the diorama materials and the ways specific events might be represented.

Closure: Remind the students to bring materials the next day.

Figure 4.7 Diorama Example

Day 2
Students will continue to research ideas, review relevant literature, and work on their dioramas.

Days 3 and 4
Students will continue work on the dioramas, cooperatively write the draft summary, edit, and write the final summary.

Day 5
Students will present, discuss, and display their dioramas. The display will be organized in chronological order to represent a visual and written timeline of the period of rapid growth in California.

Related Literature

Cobblestone: The History Magazine for Young People. "The First Transcontinental Railroad, 1869." Peterborough, NH: Cobblestone Publishers.

Cobblestone: The History Magazine for Young People. "The Pony Express: 1860–1861." Peterborough, NH: Cobblestone Publishers.

Coerr, Eleanor. (1993). *Chang's Paper Pony*. New York: HarperCollins Publishers.

Coerr, Eleanor. (1995). *Buffalo Bill and the Pony Express*. New York: HarperCollins Publishers.

Fleischman, Sid. (1988). *By the Great Horn Spoon*. New York: Little, Brown, and Company.

Holliday, J.S. (1981). *The World Rushed In: The Gold Rush Experience*. New York: Simon & Schuster.

Interact: Learning Through Involvement. *Elementary Simulations* (Catalog, 1992). Lakeside, CA. (619) 448–1474.

Levine, Ellen. (1986). *If You Traveled West in a Covered Wagon*. New York: Scholastic.

National Council for Social Studies. (Bulletin 89, 1994). *National Standards for the Social Studies* (pp. 21–30). Washington, DC: Author.

Quontamatteo, Nancy & Others. (1981). *The Gold Rush Era*. Jackson, CA: Conceptual Productions.

Rawls, Jim. (1993). *Dame Shirley and the Gold Rush*. New York: Steck-Vaughn Company.

Reinstedt, Randall. (1990). *One-Eyed Charley, The California Whip*. Carmel, CA: Ghost Town Publications.

Stewart, George. (1954). *The Pioneers Go West*. New York: Random House.

Wills, Charles A. (1994). *A Historical Album of California*. Brookfield, CT: The Millbrook Press.

Wormser, R. (1993). *The Iron Horse*. Peterborough, NH: Cobblestone Publishers.

Videocassettes:

Charlie Brown's America. The Building of the Transcontinental Railroad. (1989). Paramount Home Videos. Los Angeles.

5 Moving Westward through Literature

GRADE FIVE UNIT

Focus: United States History and Geography: Making a New Nation

LESSON TOPICS:

- Introduction to Westward Expansion
- The United States Looks toward Mexico
- The United States Expands Its Southern Border to Include Mexico
- The United States Moves into the Oregon Country
- On to Oregon
- The Mormons Move Westward
- The Effect of Westward Expansion on the Lives of Native Americans
- Westward Expansion Participants

Unit Rationale/Broad Goals

Unit Focus: *National Council for Social Studies Standards*

Strand 1. Social studies programs should include experiences that provide for the study of cultural and cultural diversity.

Strand 3. Social studies programs should include experiences that provide for the study of people, places, and environments.

Strand 5. Social studies programs should provide for the study of interation among individuals, groups, and institutions (NCSS, 1994).

This chapter has been prepared to stimulate and encourage active student involvement. The primary purpose of this unit is to provide fifth-grade students with meaningful, interrelated experiences that consider the major goals set forth by the National Council of Social Studies (1994) and by most state departments of education. An emphasis will be on the development of students' social participation skills as well as on the acquisition of factual information, problem-solving skills, and basic study skills. Specifically, the focus is on the implementation of activities that encourage students to explore literature as an avenue to a clear understanding of the events and the participants that helped set the boundaries of the United States.

Integration of Social Studies and Literature

The study of history is made more powerful and meaningful by integrating it with other subject areas. The inclusion of related literature enriches history and brings to life the events and people of the period studied. Literature has been integrated because the magic of books has been acknowledged in recent years by many curriculum specialists.

When Charlotte Crabtree (1989) wrote about the power of biographies, myths, folktales, and historical narratives, she addressed the power of literature to capture the imagination of children when she stated: "Whether these . . . are drawn from the recent past or from some long-ago reaches of human history is not the critical factor in their accessibility to children. Rather, it is the nature of the story told, its power to capture children's imagination, to draw them into the historical event or human dilemma. . . ." (page 36).

In *Children's Literature and Social Studies* (1993), Myra Zarnowski focused on the use of children's trade books and how they offer multiple perspectives related to current issues such as poverty or civil rights. She reviewed the use of introducing literature sets—a collection of books that might focus on a single current topic. These particular sets were used by children in small groups to discuss varied perspectives. Prior to group study, a brief discussion of the books in each set focused on time, place, and incidents to generate interest among the children.

The use of literature to teach social studies has been a trend in social studies instruction. According to Frederick Risinger's (1992) review of contemporary research, current curriculum guides, and other reports, this trend continues. Risinger states, "This trend has particular implications for elementary social studies. . . . Student interest is heightened when literature is used as an integral part of a social studies program. . . . [C]arefully selected literature can make historical periods come to life and provide a flavor of the thoughts and feeling surrounding a historical event" (page 2).

This chapter is intended to provide students with a sense of reality as they develop an understanding of the events and lasting changes that were occurring as a result of the movement westward in the late 1700s and throughout the mid-1800s. One meaningful way to meet this goal is to provide opportunities for students to become acquainted with literature about and by the participants involved in the westward expansion in the United States. Appropriate literature will be an integral part of instruction throughout this unit as the related events will become more vivid for the students if seen through the eyes of actual participants. The inclusion of diaries, journals, and relevant literature is intended to help students develop a deeper understanding of the diverse population that participated in America's move westward.

The overall strategy in this unit is to build bridges between other subject areas. Basic historical and geographic facts will be studied to facilitate student understanding of the events and the people who populated the expanding United States. The integration of listening, speaking, reading, writing, and basic language skills will be reinforced utilizing suggested social science content. For example, it may be possible to coordinate the reading of *Sarah, Plain and Tall* with the study of the westward movement. This reading—or other related literature—might occur concurrently or prior to the beginning of this unit.

Strategies

The teaching strategies will include the utilization of a variety of models that will best meet the instructional objectives and the diverse needs of the student population. Direct instruction of factual information and the reinforcement of specific skills will be enhanced by providing opportunities for students to collaboratively interpret history. Students will be encouraged to use their dramatic abilities as they put their efforts "on stage." Math, science, and the arts will be integrated throughout the curriculum where appropriate. Following is the description of an Advance Organizing Strategy selected used in Lesson 1 to motivate and actively involve students.

An Advance Organizing Strategy: An advance organizer has been described as a model of teaching that is "designed to increase the efficiency of information processing capabilities to absorb and relate bodies of knowledge" (Joyce & Weil, 1980, p. 10). The use of an advance organizer has been advocated by educational theorists as early as the mid-1960s. David Ausubel described advance organizers as "introductory material presented ahead of the learning task and at a higher level of abstraction and inclusiveness than the learning task itself" (Joyce & Weil, 1980, p. 81). Furthermore, Joyce and Weil described the advance organizer model as "designed to strengthen students' cognitive structures, a term Ausubel uses for a person's knowledge of a particular subject matter at any given time and how well organized, clear, and stable it is. . . . Ausubel maintains that a person's existing cognitive structure is the foremost factor governing whether new material will meaningful and how well it can be acquired and retained" (page 77).

Based on the work of educational theorists and curriculum specialists, the use of an advance organizer appears to be an effective strategy that can provide students the structured input necessary to help them learn new and more specific information in a subsequent unit of study.

An advance organizer utilizing literature has been used as a strategy in some lessons to set the stage for the subsequent in-depth unit of study. For example, an advance organizer was implemented to set the stage for an upcoming unit focusing on Moving Westward through Literature. The strategy used in Lesson 1 was included to elicit student interest and prepare students for the events and people they will encounter as they explore the westward movement. Literature and maps were used to provide students with a brief glimpse of the events and participants in the historical period that will be closely examined during the subsequent learning experiences. An overhead projector was used to provide visuals as the students were introduced to each event. Transparencies made from book covers visually illustrated people and events. The advance organizer continues to set the stage for the subsequent unit of study. As a closure for this advance organizer, the teacher elicits student thought by asking them to indicate—verbally and in writing—what they hope to learn more about during the subsequent unit of study.

Overall Evaluation

Student progress and needs will be determined by using a combination of evaluative and assessment tools. The lessons in this unit encourage an ongoing assessment in which instruction and assessment are integrated. The lesson activities allow for assessment that provides the student with immediate feedback and provides the teacher with information to make decisions about the appropriateness of subsequent student activities. An eclectic approach to assessment can include observations, student folders, student projects, student presentations, and student essays reactions. Due to the difficulty in developing and assessing student essay tests, the following example provided will help the teacher determine essay questions and develop a uniform scoring system. This example is appropriate to assess previously studied information and events focused on in Lesson 2, which were intended to indicate examples of events and were not intended to indicate a priority of importance.

Essay Question Directions

1. Please read carefully the following information:

   During the 1800s events occurred that led to a conflict between the United States and Mexico. Consider the below indicated events:

Mexico wins independence from Spain.	Mexico offers land grants to anyone bringing settlers to Mexico.	Mexico outlaws slavery and stops further American settlement in Mexico.	Santa Anna becomes dictator of Mexico.

2. Select two of the above events and write your essay about them.

   Students may earn a total of 30 points. The awarding of points will be determined by the inclusion and accuracy of the following requested information.

3. Please include in your essay the following information:

   - A description of each selected event and the time frame in which each event occurred.

   - Discuss how the two events are related.

   - Discuss how the events led to the conflict with Mexico.

The following questions are included to illustrate standards that will help the teacher assess essays and determine the points earned by specific student responses:

- Did the student address all the information requested by the teacher?
- Is the information requested discussed in depth and does it include examples that support ideas and conclusions?
- Does the essay include accurate information and knowledge of the selected events discussed?
- Is the requested information presented in a sequential, well-organized, and clearly written manner?

Points will be subtracted from the total possible points that students can earn if the essay responses do not answer all information requested by the teacher, indicate limited understanding, contain historical errors, and lack depth.

This unit focuses on a limited number of events; however, the ideas are presented to serve as catalysts for teachers. The omission of specific events or people was not meant to diminish their importance or contributions. The ideas presented and the people represented are intended to be examples that will encourage each teacher to utilize his or her expertise and specific interests to include equally important events and participants. The unit could be expanded to focus in depth on selected topics and/or include other important aspects of westward expansion.

References

California Department of Education. (January, 1994). *A Sampler of History-Social Science Assessment* (pp. 30, 32), Sacramento, CA: Author.

Crabtree, Charlotte. (Winter, 1989). History is for children. *American Educator*, pp. 34–39.

Joyce, B., & Weil, M. (1980). *Models of Teaching* (2nd ed.). Englewood Cliffs, NJ: Prentice Hall.

National Council for Social Studies. (Bulletin 89, 1994). *Curriculum Standards for the Social Studies* (pp. 21–30). Washington, DC: Author.

Risinger, Frederick C. (1992). *Trends in K–12 Social Studies*. Clearinghouse for Social Studies/Social Science Education, Bloomington, IN, EDO-SO-92-8. Washington, DC: Office of Educational Research and Improvement ED).

Zarnowski, Myra. (1993). Using literature sets to promote conversation about social studies topics." *Children's Literature and Social Studies*, pp. 35–41.

Lesson 1: Introduction to Westward Expansion

Time Frame: 1 to 3 days

Materials/Equipment: *Sarah, Plain and Tall* (MacLachlan), *Sacagawea* (Brown), *The Incredible Journey of Lewis and Clark* (Blumberg), overhead transparencies, large U.S. map, individual U.S. outline maps (see page 75), overhead projector.

Broad Objective: The students will understand that specific events occurring in the United States during the early 1800s hastened settlement of land beyond the Mississippi River.

Specific Objective: After a general review of the Louisiana Purchase and the Lewis and Clark Expedition and after exposure to relevant literature, the students will:

1. Develop an awareness of the major events and the people that opened the way for settlement across the Mississippi River.
2. Indicate on individual maps the boundaries of the Louisiana Purchase, and the Lewis and Clark routes (see Figures 5.1, 5.2, 5.3 on pp. 76–78).
3. Begin Westward Expansion folders.

Anticipatory Set/Motivation: (A large United States outline map will be the focal point of a bulletin board. Relevant information will be added to the map during the course of this unit.) Make a bridge from past learning by eliciting a class discussion about a book, *Sarah, Plain and Tall*, that had been recently read by the class. Discuss Sarah Wheaton's reason for her journey from Maine to her new home on the prairie. Indicate the approximate route and mileage on the large map. Read excerpts from *Sarah, Plain and Tall* to illustrate Sarah's personal traits and the reason she traveled westward. (One excerpt might be Sarah's letter in response to Jacob's advertisement for a wife.) Remind the students that Sarah is a contemporary pioneer who faced uncertainties as she moved westward in search of a new life.

Lesson Procedure: This lesson will be presented in the form of an advance organizer to introduce the study of Westward Expansion.

Input: "Many years before Sarah's journey, events began to happen that encouraged people to settle on land beyond the Mississippi River. Today we are going to begin the study of a period in American history in which the United States began to expand its borders. It was a time in which people with various needs and thoughts began to populate what is now the western and southwestern areas of the United States. We will read stories about a variety of people, their reasons for migration, and the trails they took as they traveled westward. Like Sarah, they had specific reasons for their migration westward across the Mississippi River. As a result, the trails they chose and their subsequent experiences were quite different."

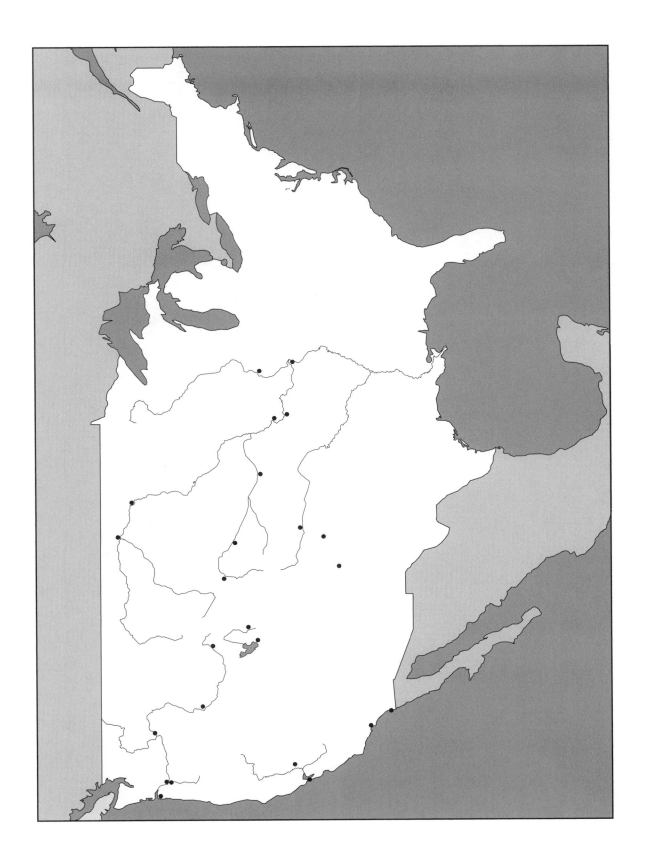

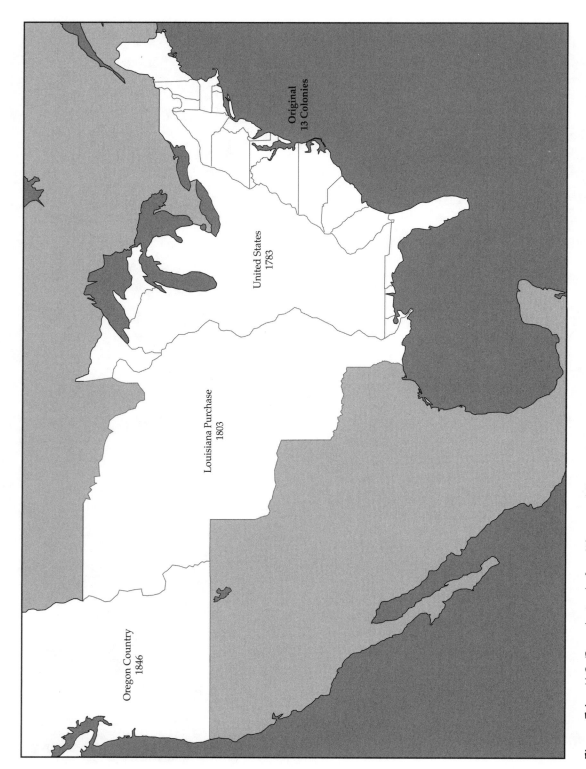

Figure 5.1 *U.S. Boundaries before Westward Expansion*

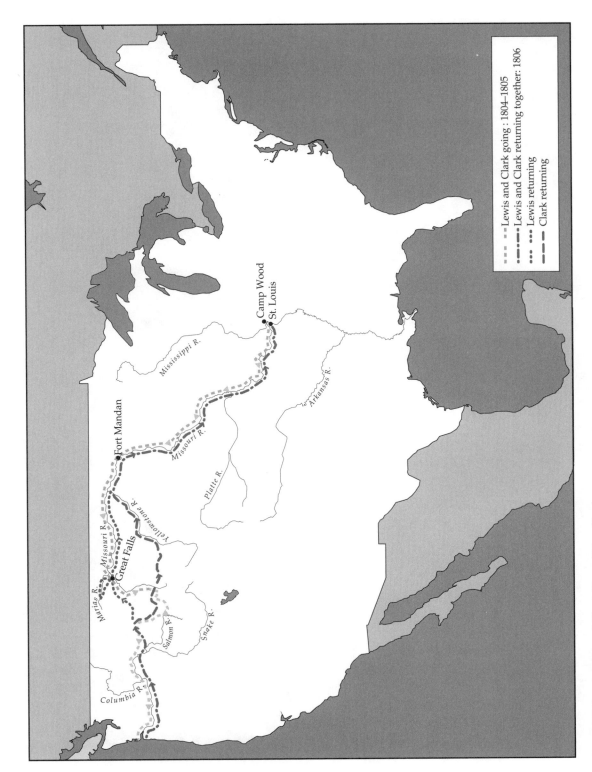

Figure 5.2 Lewis and Clark Expedition Routes

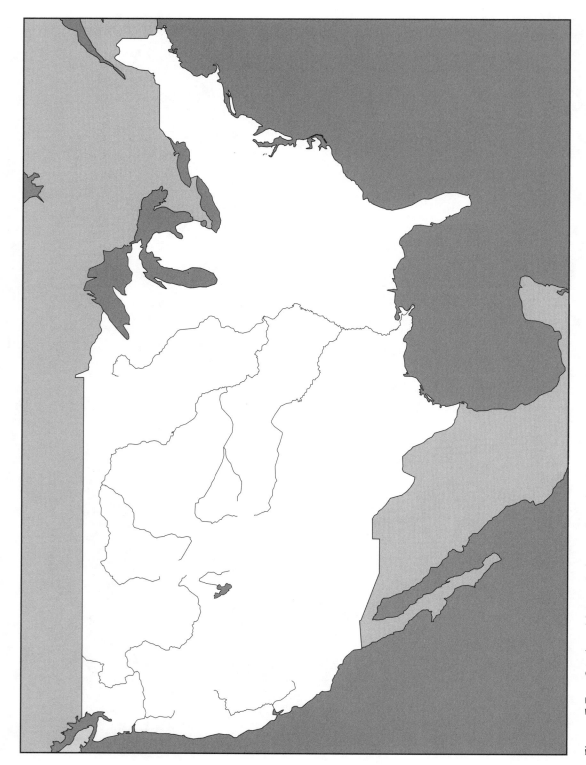

Figure 5.3   Student Map to Indicate Specific Trails

To help the students understand the initial opening of the unknown land west of the Mississippi River, the teacher will review knowledge gained from a previous unit focusing on the growth of a new nation. The teacher will focus on a review of the Louisiana Purchase and the subsequent Lewis and Clark Expedition. The boundaries of the Louisiana Purchase will be indicated on the large U.S. map.

Excerpts from *The Incredible Journey of Lewis and Clark* (Blumberg) and from *Sacagawea* (Brown) will be read to bring to life the actual experiences of the participants while exploring the areas west of the Mississippi River. Excerpts chosen will illustrate the personal qualities of Lewis, Clark, and Sacagawea. The teacher may choose to focus on Sacagawea and make comparisons to other women of the west. During the readings the teacher may focus on the routes taken by Lewis and Clark by indicating specific landmarks on the large map. Additionally, the teacher might visually reinforce story ideas by writing major events in diary form on the board or on chart paper.

Modeling/Guided Practice: After the readings the teacher will provide students with outline maps. (Examples of all maps are available throughout this chapter.) The teacher will focus and guide students by using an overhead projector and outline map transparencies. The teacher will elicit student input and guide students as they draw boundaries of the Louisiana Purchase and the route taken by Lewis and Clark as they explored the unknown territory. Story excerpts will provide additional guidance as the students begin their individual maps. (Pages 10–11 in the Blumberg book are especially helpful in tracing the Lewis and Clark Trail.)

Independent Practice: The students will be given the opportunity to write the previously outlined major events in diary form. This will become part of their unit folder.

Closure: The teacher will remind the students that this lesson is an overview and the beginning of a unit of study in which the causes and effects of Westward Expansion will be investigated in depth. Map development, writing journals, and note taking are ongoing activities. Maps and information relevant to subsequent lessons will be included in the individual student folders.

A Lesson Extension Idea: The students might develop simple cinquains in which they use Sacagawea and Sarah as subjects. (See sample ideas in the following box.) If the cinquain form is new to the students, a lesson might be developed to teach then how to write cinquains. The book *Sacagawea* will be helpful in providing an insight into the character of Sacagawea and reveal experiences that bring realism to the story of Lewis and Clark as they explored the land the unknown west.

A simple cinquain:

Line 1........One noun (title)

Line 2........Two adjectives describing the title

Line 3........Three verbs (-ing words) related to the title

Line 4........A four-word phrase describing or commenting on the title

Line 5........A noun—synonym or antonym for the title

Example:

Sarah	Sacagawea
tall, plain	quick, graceful
singing, painting, caring	daring, seeking, helping
a woman moving westward	a guide through wilderness
Pioneer	Bird Woman

Lesson 2: The United States Looks toward Mexico

Time Frame: 1 to 3 days

Materials/Equipment: *Tree in the Trail* (Holling), *Susanna of the Alamo* (Jakes), *The Santa Fe Trail: Dangers and Dreams* (Kurtz), outline maps, overhead projector, social studies text, chart paper.

Broad Objective: Students will develop an understanding of the events that led to the settlement and acquisition of Texas.

Specific Objective: After factual input from text and maps and reading excerpts from related literature, the students will complete an event/effect journal related to events leading to the conflict with Mexico.

Anticipatory Set: "Yesterday we read about and discussed the exploration that opened the way for future settlement in western portions of the United States. However, many years earlier trappers traveled to the southwest by way of the Santa Fe Trail. (Find and draw on the large bulletin board map.) Today we will discover why people traveled the Santa Fe Trail (see Figure 5.4) and the events that led to the conflict with Mexico."

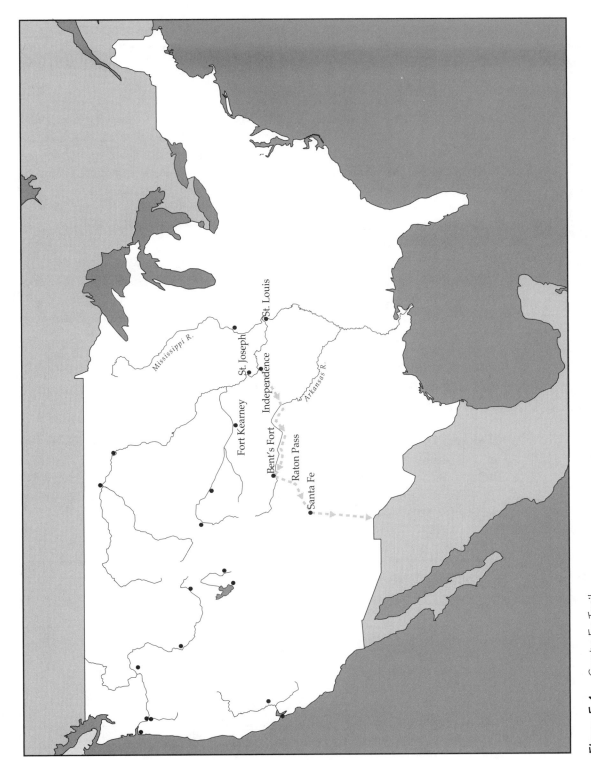

Figure 5.4 *Santa Fe Trail*

Input/Modeling: Read excerpts from *Tree in the Trail* and/or *The Santa Fe Trail*. Focus on the early trappers and their use of the Santa Fe Trail as a two-way route. The Santa Fe Trail has an interesting story to tell of events that led to the eventual settlement of Americans in the southwest.

As the *Tree in the Trail* is read, the teacher will model the development of a chronological list of events/effects told through the eyes of a tree. This might be done on an overhead or the board to provide both audio and visual input. Additionally, the teacher will use the social studies text, question, and guide reading to elicit factual information that led to the populating and acquisition of Texas. During the reading a chronological list of events will be developed.

Guided Practice/Modeling: After the reading, the teacher will model one or two examples of locating events and guide the students to determine the effect of that event. The teacher will choose examples, elicit answers from students, and model this procedure using an overhead projector or chart paper. The students will be introduced to a event/effect paper (see box at bottom of this page) of events leading to the conflict with Mexico. The process of completing the first event will be modeled by the teacher.

Independent Activity: The students will complete the event/effect paper using the social studies text and literature. They will draw the Santa Fe Trail on their personal maps.

Closure: The students will share their results. As a closure for this lesson, the teacher might read the first few pages of *Susanna of the Alamo*, which illustrate the thoughts of Susanna as the Mexican army began to surround the old mission. The reactions of the students will serve to lead into the next lesson about the events at the Alamo.

Event and Effect Journal

Event	Effect
1821	
Mexico wins independence from Spain. Texas is part of the new nation.	One example: Mexico wanted to strengthen itself as a country. Few people wanted to move to Texas.
1823	
Mexico offers land grants to anyone, bringing settlers to Mexico.	

1830

Mexico outlaws slavery. This stops
further Americans from immigrating
to Mexico.

1834

Santa Anna becomes dictator
of Mexico.

Lesson 3: The United States Expands
Its Southern Border to Include Mexico

Time Frame: 2 to 3 days

Materials/Equipment: *Susanna of the Alamo* (Jakes), *Make Way for Sam Houston* (Fritz), picture of the Alamo, Alamo transparency and patterns, outline maps, social studies text.

Broad Objective: The students will understand major events leading to the setting of the southern border of the United States.

Specific Objective: After reading pertinent literature and factual information, each small group of students will write one response to an event related to the acquisition of Texas.

Anticipatory Set: (Tape large picture of the Alamo on the chalkboard.) "Yesterday, we began to experience the story of the Alamo as seen through the eyes of Susanna Dickenson." (Review the past reading and elicit student responses. Write their responses and vocabulary around the picture of the Alamo on the chalkboard. See Figure 5.5 on p. 84.)

Stated Purpose: "Much of what we know about the Alamo has been told by those who experienced that historical event. If the Alamo could talk, it would reveal a great deal about the people and events that led to the acquisition of Texas by the United States. Today we will continue to learn about events that resulted in setting the southern boundary of the United States. Later we will write about those events and develop a story about Texas."

Input/Modeling: "Our story might begin with information about the Alamo." (The teacher and students will continue reading excerpts from *Susanna of the*

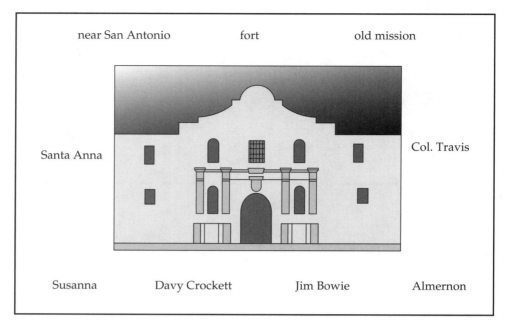

Figure 5.5   *Alamo Discussion Example*

Alamo to provide students with the necessary information. The teacher will model an example event/response to prepare the students for the subsequent independent activity. The students will take notes that will be helpful when they research and write their responses. The students will be exposed to other primary sources—such as *Make Way for Sam Houston*—in addition to the social studies text.)

Guided Practice: To encourage active student involvement and to assure success during the group activity, the teacher will model an additional event/response statement on the overhead projector before the group activity begins. The teacher will guide the class as they locate and provide appropriate responses for a specific events. The teacher will write their responses using a double entry format as an example and to provide an opportunity to practice locating appropriate responses. (See the event/response example for sample topics in the box on pages 85–86.)

Group Activity: After the students have practiced under the guidance of the teacher, they will work in small groups or pairs as they develop responses to specific events. These responses will be written in a double-entry format. Groups will each be provided a specific event chosen from the event/response page and resource ideas to help them as they research their topics.

Closure: Each group will present its efforts to the class in a logical sequence. After the students present their stories, the teacher will summarize and point out the boundary changes on the large map and indicate territorial acquisition by using an overhead transparency. The students will make these changes on their maps.

Extended Activity: A time line is an effective way of presenting time spans. This could be developed as part of the summary. The time line should represent events that occurred between the Battle at the Alamo in 1836 and the Gadsden Purchase in 1853. Example events 1836 through 1853 could be written and illustrated on butcher paper as in the following box.

Examples:

Events	Responses
February 23–March 5, 1836 Battle at the Alamo	American settlers sought revenge. The battle cry became "Remember the Alamo."
April 21, 1836 Battle at San Jacinto	The Texas army led by Sam Houston defeated the Mexican Army.
1836 Texas becomes an independent nation.	Sam Houston became the first president of the new Texas Republic.
Texas asked to be admitted United States.	Some people in Texas owned slaves. The United States contained thirteen free and thirteen slave states. Making Texas a state would upset that balance.
1845 Texas becomes a state.	Mexico became angry and refused to negotiate with the United States.
1846 The U.S. president ordered troops to the Rio Grande River.	April 1846: Mexican and American troops fought a battle. This began the war with Mexico.

Events	Responses
April 1846 War begins at the Rio Grande River.	American General Taylor crossed the Rio Grande River and won several victories. General Scott captured Mexico city in 1847.
February 1848 The Treaty of Guadalupe Hidalgo was signed.	The United States paid Mexico $15 million for the lands it received after the Mexican War. The lands included California, Nevada, Utah, most of New Mexico and Arizona, and parts of Wyoming and Colorado. The Rio Grande River was established as the boundary between Mexico and the United States.
1853 Gadsden Purchase.	The United States paid $10 million for land in the southern part of New Mexico and Arizona. The southern border of the United States is set.

Lesson 4: The United States Moves into the Oregon Country

Time Frame: 1 to 3 days

Materials/Equipment: *The Story of the Oregon Trail* (Stein), *Westward Expansion* (Mitchell & Moehle), social studies text, outline maps, transparencies made from time line and maps.

Broad Objective: The students will gain an understanding of the people and events that encouraged movement into the Oregon Country.

Specific Objective: After reading and discussing relevant literature, the students will create and label a pictorial time line that illustrates movement into Oregon Country. They will also write their predictions of life on the Oregon Trail and outline the route on their individual maps.

Anticipatory Set: "During our previous inquiry into America's move west of the Mississippi River, the focus was on the settlement and acquisition of Texas. The terms of the Treaty of Guadalupe Hidalgo and subsequent land acquisitions expanded the U.S. territory in the southwest." (Review map using an overhead and large wall map. Elicit student volunteers to point out the Rio Grande as the southern border and the states acquired by treaty and purchase.)

Input: "In the early 1820s and 1830s while pioneers were encouraged to settle the Mexican province of Texas, the northwest part of the United States was being explored by trappers and missionaries. This area was referred to as the Oregon Country. The early exploration into this area encouraged others to set out on the Oregon Trail for a variety of reasons."

As the teacher guides the students through relevant literature, the route and landmarks will be indicated using a transparency on an overhead projector. The transparencies can be made from the outline maps. Additionally, the focus will be on gleaning important facts from relevant literature. The following information will be outlined as a guide for the subsequent time line (Figures 5.6 and 5.7 on pp. 88–89):

1. The Louisiana Purchase (1803)
2. Lewis and Clark Expedition (1804-1806)
3. Trappers and fur traders journeyed to Oregon via the Oregon Trail
4. John Jacob Astor established a fur-trading outpost in Oregon Country (Astoria, 1811).
5. By the 1830s only Great Britain and the United States competed for control of the Oregon Country.
6. Missionaries began entering Oregon Country.
   a. Marcus Whitman and his wife, Narcissa (1836)
7. In 1843 the first of the great wagon trains left Independence, Missouri. This marked the beginning of the mass movement into Oregon Country.
8. In 1846, the United States and Great Britain agreed the 49th parallel will be the northern boundary of the United States.

Guided Practice/Modeling: Provide each student with a United States outline map. Using a transparency made from the outline map, the teacher will guide the students as they outline the Oregon Country, Oregon Trail, important points, and the eventual northern boundary at the 49th parallel (see Figures 5.8 and 5.9 on pp. 90–91).

The teacher will model the beginning of a pictorial time line illustrating the opening of the Oregon Country for settlement. (Time line transparencies can be made from the time line examples.)

Independent Practice: Students will complete the time line that will become part of their folders. The students will write a paragraph about how they might feel if they were preparing for a journey into the unknown. The teacher will

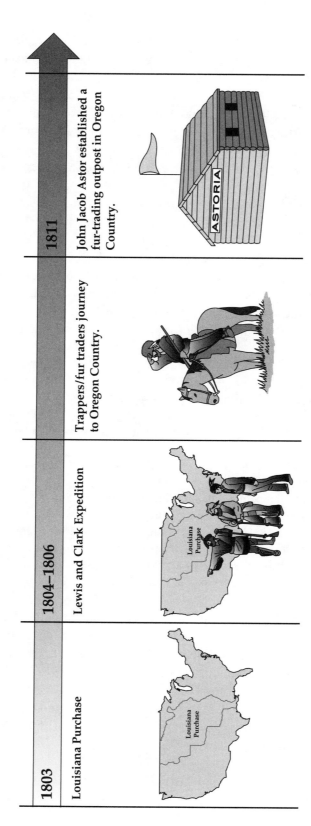

1803	1804–1806		1811
Louisiana Purchase	Lewis and Clark Expedition	Trappers/fur traders journey to Oregon Country.	John Jacob Astor established a fur-trading outpost in Oregon Country.

Figure 5.6   Time Line Ideas: 1803–1811

1830	1836	1843	1846
Great Britain and United States compete for control of Oregon Country.	Missionaries began entering Oregon Country (Marcus Whitman and his wife, Narcissa.)	The first of the great wagon trains left Independence, Missouri. Began the mass movement into Oregon Country.	U.S. and Great Britain agreed that the 49th parallel will be the northern boundary of United States.

Oregon Country claimed by the United States and Great Britain

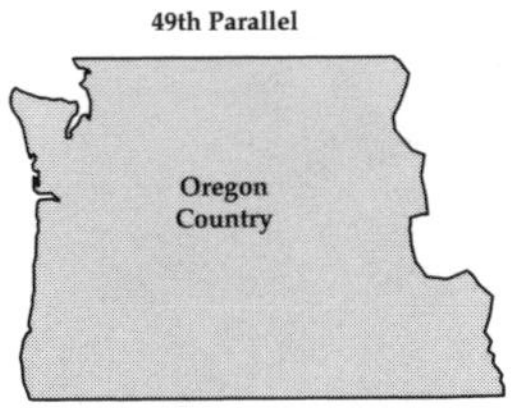

49th Parallel

Oregon Country

Figure 5.7 *Time Line Ideas: 1830–1846*

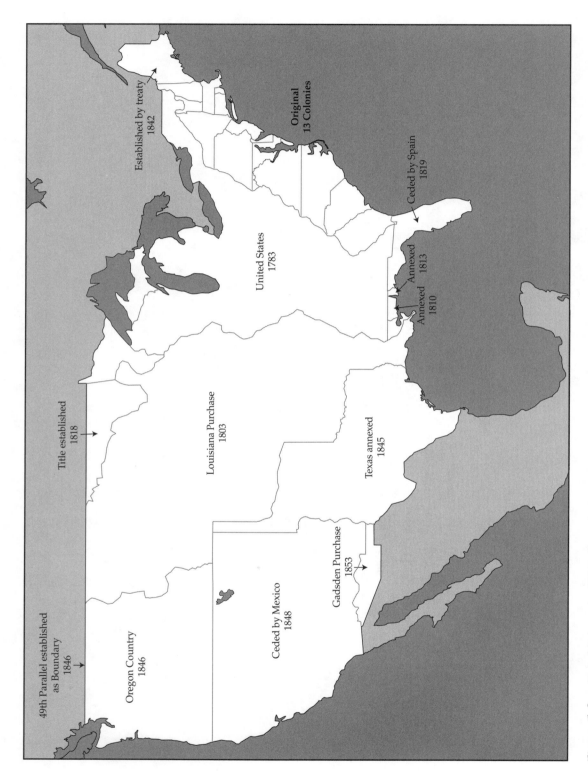

Figure 5.8 *Establishment of U.S. Boundaries*

49th Parallel established as Boundary 1846

Title established 1818

Oregon Country 1846

Established by treaty 1842

Louisiana Purchase 1803

United States 1783

Original 13 Colonies

Ceded by Spain 1819

Annexed 1813

Annexed 1810

Ceded by Mexico 1848

Gadsden Purchase 1853

Texas annexed 1845

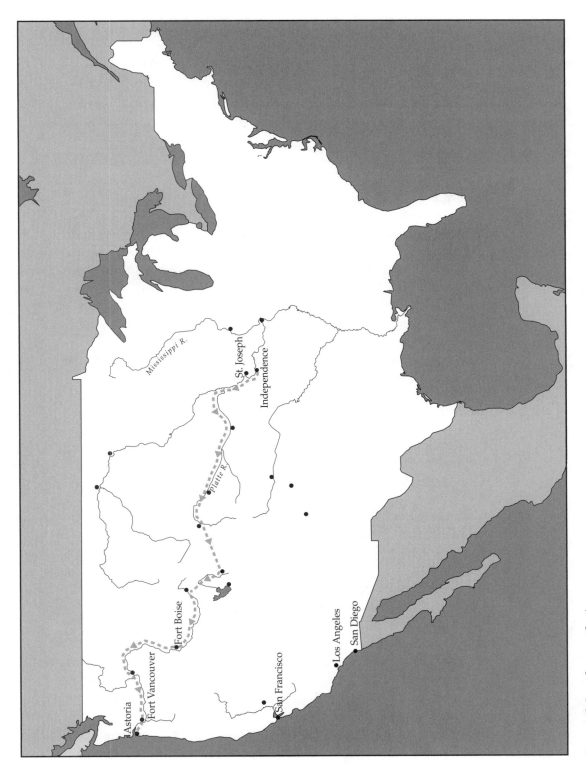

Figure 5.9 *Oregon Trail*

assess student knowledge about the necessary arrangements for the journey by using the previously discussed three-point scoring system.

Closure: The students will share their concerns about life on the Oregon Trail. This discussion will set the stage for the next lesson—On to Oregon.

Lesson 5: On to Oregon

Time Frame: 3 to 4 days

Materials/Equipment: *Wagons West* (Chambers), *The Oregon Trail* (Fisher), *If You Traveled West in a Covered Wagon* (Levine), *Women's Diaries of the Westward Journey* (Schlissel), *The Story of the Oregon Trail* (Stein), *Westward Expansion* (Mitchell & Moehle), *The Oregon Trail* (Kurtz), excerpts about specific events, task cards, summary squares for the quilt, overhead projector, chart paper.

Broad Objective: The students will gain an understanding of the necessary journey preparations, and the subsequent life on the Oregon Trail.

Specific Objective: After reading pertinent literature, the students will:

1. Summarize and illustrate specific events related to the Oregon Trail.
2. Combine their event summaries to form a class patchwork quilt that tells a story of life on the Oregon Trail.

Anticipatory Set: Elicit responses concerning who these people might be and why they chose to travel westward. The teacher will make a bridge from the previous lesson by eliciting student responses related to their predictions about life on the Oregon Trail. "For the next few days we will read about the actual experiences of those venturing into the unknown. Later these ideas will be helpful as we write summaries and illustrate life on the Oregon Trail."

Input/Modeling: "These experiences may be similar to the uncertainties faced by many settlers who left their homes to start new lives in the northwest." Choose one of the books listed at the beginning of this lesson, draw a large circle on the board, write the book title inside the circle, and elicit student thoughts about the book.

During the discussion ask questions such as: "What do you think the setting is like?" "Why?" Ask for rationale and focus on critical thinking skills. Elicit descriptive language about the characters, setting, and possible events. Cluster responses around the title on the board. Encourage the students to keep these ideas in mind so they can compare their ideas with the actual happenings. During and after excerpts from the book are read, elicit student input, reinforce major concepts, and add to or change ideas that were written on the board during the initial brainstorming.

Guided Practice/Modeling: After reading excerpts, choose one event, setting, or character and guide the students as they develop a summary of that event—such as preparing for the journey. This might be modeled on chart paper or on the overhead projector. See the example in Figure 5.10. Discuss other topics that might be part of life on the Oregon Trail. Possible topics could be mapping the journey, loading wagons, cooking/eating on the trail, children and/or women and their responsibilities, dangers on the trail, geography/climate, specific events, and characters.

Group Activity: Groups of three students will draft a summary about a specific event. To assure that major events will be summarized, the teacher will develop

Preparation for the Journey to Oregon

The purchase of a strong covered wagon was usually the first task for the pioneers as they prepared for the journey to Oregon. Some of the earliest pioneers used the sturdy Conestoga wagon. Later most pioneers chose a smaller, lighter wagon that was about 14 to 15 feet in length. The covered wagon was a wagon with a canvas top that was rubbed with oil to make it waterproof.

Covered wagons were often called "prairie schooners." This was because the big white canvas cover looked like a large sail. When the wagon crossed the high prairie grass, the wheels were often hidden. This made the wagon look like a big boat sailing across the prairie.

Figure 5.10 Preparation for the Journey to Oregon

task cards that indicate a specific topic suggested above and a list of appropriate resources. The final summary and illustration will be on paper squares.

Closure: The students will share their summaries. The summary squares will be combined to form a class patchwork quilt that tells a story of life on the Oregon Trail. This project will be displayed in the classroom.

Lesson Extensions: After viewing the video, *Seven Alone*, the students could write a sequel for the story that illustrates possible events after the children settled in their new home in Oregon. This activity might be presented using a writing workshop format.

Lesson 6: The Mormons Move Westward

Time Frame: 1 to 2 days

Materials/Equipment: *The Mormon Church: A Basic History* (Hughes), *Westward Expansion* (Mitchell & Moehle), double-entry journal format.

Broad Objective: The students will understand that some people moved westward for religious reasons.

Specific Objective: After reading relevant literature, the students will react to specific excerpts using a double-entry journal and add information to their personal maps about the travels of the Mormons (Figure 5.11).

Anticipatory Set: "In previous lessons many of the people traveled west because of opportunities for land or gold; however, some people moved because of their religious beliefs. During the study of early America, we discovered that other groups moved because of religious intolerance. (Roger Williams established the colony of Rhode Island because of Puritan intolerance in Massachusetts.) The Mormons are an example of a group that moved because of their religious beliefs during the time of westward expansion in the United States."

Input: The teacher will discuss the story of the Mormons, their leaders, and their purpose for leaving their homes to build new lives in the area that is now Utah. The teacher will add the Mormon trail and other relevant landmarks to the large bulletin board. Excerpts from *The Mormon Church* and from *Westward Expansion* will be read to provide realism and understanding as the Mormons find a place to settle—the Salt Lake City area.

Modeling/Guided Practice: After the readings, the teacher will choose a relevant excerpt to model a student written reaction using a double-entry journal format.

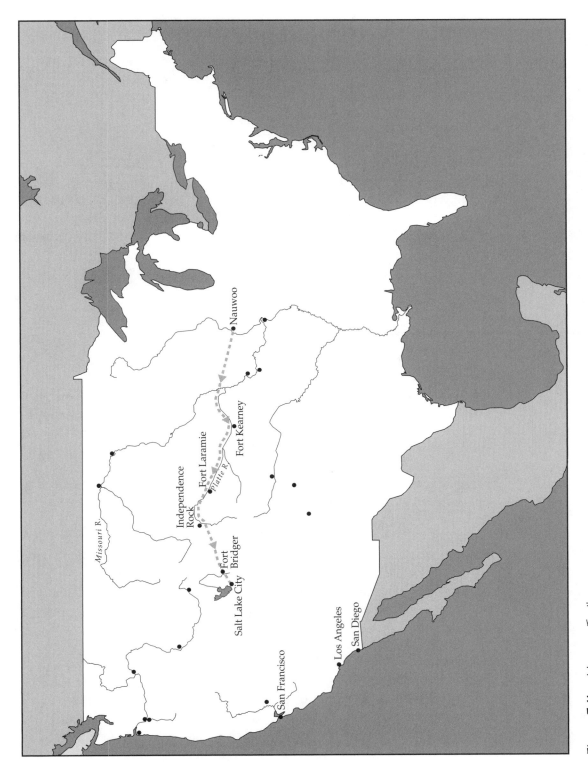

Figure 5.11   Mormon Trail

Independent Practice: The teacher will then provide students excerpts/ideas from the stories to which they can react. Here is one example:

Question	*Student Response*
What did the seagulls have to do with the final settlement of the Mormons?	

Closure: The teacher will ask for student volunteers to share their reactions with the class. The teacher will encourage the students to summarize their ideas and reinforce the idea that people moved westward for a variety of reasons. The double-entry journal and the map will be part of the individual folders. Additionally, the students will indicate relevant trails, landmarks, and towns on their personal maps (as modeled on the large bulletin board map).

Lesson 7: Westward Expansion: The Effect on the Lives of Native Americans

Time Frame: 3 to 4 days

Materials/Equipment: *Brother Eagle, Sister Sky* (Jeffers), social studies text (Houghton Mifflin), *The Indians* (Time-Life Books), *Atlas of American History* (Rand McNally), *Only the Name Remains: The Cherokees and the Trail of Tears* (Bealer), *The Defenders* (McGovern), *The American Reader* (Ravitch), maps.

Broad Objective: The students will gain an understanding of the reactions of Native Americans and the changes in their lives as a result of Westward Expansion in the United States.

Specific Objective: After teacher input, readings, and class discussions, the students will write news articles about events and opinions that focus on the treatment of Native Americans during the period of Westward Expansion. The students are expected to include factual information and statements supporting their opinions.

Anticipatory Set: "As the United States expanded its border from ocean to ocean, some groups of people were being displaced from their homelands." (Discuss some of the concerns of the Native Americans and their perceptions about nature and the land in which they live. This discussion will be reinforced by reading *Brother Eagle, Sister Sky*. This could be compared with Chief Seattle's speech from *The American Reader*.)

Stated Purpose: "During the next few days we are going to discuss specific people and events that changed the lives of Native Americans as settlers moved westward across the expanding United States. Later you will write newspaper articles about those events and the subsequent reactions. To help you with this task, we will review events, governmental policies, and reactions concerning the treatment of Native Americans."

Input: The following topics will be discussed and written on the board. The students will participate in the readings and discussions. The facts will be reinforced as the students outline pertinent information that will be helpful when they write the subsequent article.

A. Native Americans React to Encroachment on Tribal Lands
   1. Tecumseh (Excerpts from *The Defenders*; SS text)
   2. Osceola (Excerpts from *The Defenders*; SS text)
   3. Sequoyah
      a. Focus on the period of 1815–1830 in which the Cherokees attempt to live peacefully with the settlers (SS text; *Sequoyah* [Cwiklik]).
B. Governmental policy regarding Native Americans
   1. Formation of Bureau of Indian Affairs (1824)
   2. Indian Removal Policy
      a. Discuss and outline the Trail of Tears
         (Read excerpts from *Only the Name Remains: The Cherokees and the Trail of Tears*)
C. Impact on Plains Indians
   1. Infringement on basic needs: buffalo/ grasslands
   2. Illnesses
   3. Governmental intervention

Modeling/Guided Practice: "If you had lived during the time in which the United States was expanding westward, how might you describe the effect it had on the lives of Native Americans? Based on the readings and discussions, opinions and reactions concerning the treatment of Native Americans appeared to vary due to the diversity of thought and needs. Today we will begin to write articles that include realistic descriptions and supporting statements concerning the events and reactions that changed the lives of Native Americans during the period of westward expansion." (Provide examples from current newspapers and model article format [who, what, where, when, why, and result of the event or action].)

Group Activity

1. Each group will be given a *task card* that includes a *topic* (Sequoyah, Trail of Tears, Plains Indians, Removal Policy, etc.) and *resource ideas*.
2. Each group will decide on individual responsibilities and tasks (recorder, spokesperson, etc.).
3. Each group member will provide input as the draft copy is written, discussed, revised, and rewritten in the final form.

Closure: The articles will be presented by the reporter to the entire class. The final articles will be displayed on a bulletin board in the form of a newspaper front page.

Provide for Differences: Motivating literature is selected to encourage and help children at various reading levels learn about the concerns of Native Americans during Westward Expansion. The teaching strategies chosen are intended to provide students with opportunities to function using a preferred modality. Group activities are intended to provide students with opportunities to become responsible as they gain knowledge collaboratively.

Lesson 8: Westward Expansion Participants

Time Frame: 3 to 4 days

Materials/Equipment: Social studies text, encyclopedias, related literature, task cards, biographies, maps, chart paper, Rand McNally *Atlas of American History*, *Tree in the Trail* (Holling).

Broad Objective: The students will understand that purpose, conditions, events, and affects are unique for specific groups who participated in America's Westward Expansion.

Specific Objective: During cooperative group inquiry, each group will gather, organize, and summarize data related to one group of people that participated or were affected by Westward Expansion. Based on the result of their findings, each group will accept, reject, or modify class-stated hypotheses.

Anticipatory Set (Motivation): "Prior lessons indicated that diverse people, utilizing a variety of trails, participated in the movement westward." (Review the map indicating the time frame and trails during Westward Expansion of the United States, 1800 to mid-1800s.) Let me read an excerpt indicating specific historical events related to the Santa Fe Trail. This trail is unique in purpose and in the people that chose this path. (Read from *Tree in the Trail*). This reading is about specific people who participated in or were affected by America's movement westward. Do you think the motivation and subsequent events are similar to other groups involved in westward expansion?"

Check for Understanding: Questioning occurs throughout the lesson to direct the inquiry procedure and to check for understanding.

Lesson Procedure (Cooperative Group Inquiry)

1. *Problem Definition:* "In prior lessons an overview of the diverse groups involved in westward expansion indicated people began to move westward in search of a new or different life."

What conditions or events motivated specific groups of people to move westward? How did specific groups influence or affect the native people or region in which they moved?

2. *Hypothesizing:* These questions prompt students to react. The teacher draws attention to specific groups of people and their differences in motivation, purpose, and choice of trails as they moved westward. The teacher will elicit student opinion and generalizations during discussion in an attempt to help students state their hypotheses. (Conditions and/or events motivated specific groups of people to move westward. Second, specific groups did affect the native people and the region to which they moved.) Responses will be charted.

3. *Exploration:* As the students become aware of the differences in their reactions, the teacher will guide them in structuring the inquiry. The teacher will guide the students into outlining the persons and topics they will explore to help their research. Exploration may require one or two days. The following are example topics for exploration: Lewis and Clark Expedition, the Alamo, Jedediah Smith, Oregon Trail, Black Heroes of the Wild West, Pioneer Women, and Native American leaders. The teacher will guide the class into listing research questions such as:
   - Describe the topic (What is it? or Who is it?).
   - Time and place in which the person lived.
   - Time and location if topic is a trail.
   - Why is the topic or person important?
   - What happened as a result of this person's actions?
   - What major events took place on or as a result of the specified trail?
   - Add other important information you might wish to report.

4. *Grouping:* Groups are formed based on interest and by teacher direction. Appropriate task cards will be given, individual group members will be delegated specific responsibilities, and the students will plan and decide what resources are needed to answer the research questions. (The teacher will direct and guide the students in using the school as well as outside resources.) Each group member will carry out his or her assignment. This will occur independently as well as in groups. The students will be given the opportunity to begin planning the research the first day. Those working together will be guided into formulating and beginning the research in class, coordinate their efforts, and plan for that evening's independent research. Each student will gather data based on his/her task assignment.

5. *Data Analysis:* The individual group members will report back to their group to inform others of the progress made in their research efforts. Students will organize the data and determine its correctness and usefulness. The data will be interpreted and summarized.

6. *Reaching a Conclusion:* Based on the research data gathered, each group will accept, reject, or modify the stated hypotheses: *Conditions or events motivate specific groups of people to move westward. Specific groups influence or affect the native people or region to which they moved.*

Unit Culmination: In subsequent days the students will plan a group presentation for the entire class. Each group will present its findings in a manner of its choosing. Ideas for presentations may be a research paper, play, story roll, diorama, poem, or mural. All findings and presentations will be assessed/ evaluated according to accuracy and completeness of data. A three-point guide will be helpful to use as a tool.

While planning presentations, the students will have opportunities to provide and accept assistance within groups. They will become involved in audio, visual, and kinesthetic modes of learning in an effort to meet the various differences in learning. The speakers with limited English will have numerous non-threatening opportunities to develop oral and written language skills.

Related Literature

Atlas of American History. (1991). Skokie, IL: Rand McNally

Allen, T.D. (Ed.) (1974). *Arrows Four: Prose and Poetry by Young American Indians.* New York: Washington Square Press

Anderson, Joan. (1989). *Spanish Pioneers of the Southwest.* New York: E.P. Dutton.

Bealer, Alex. (1972). *Only the Names Remain: The Cherokees and the Trail of Tears.* Little, Brown.

Blumberg, Rhoda. (1987). *The Incredible Journey of Lewis & Clark.* New York: Lothrop, Lee & Shepard Books.

Brown, Marian Marsh. (1988). *Sacagawea.* Chicago: Childrens Press.

Chambers, Catherine E. (1984). *Wagons West: Off to Oregon.* Mahwah, NJ: Troll Associates.

Drumm, Stella M. (Ed.). (1982). *Down the Santa Fe Trail and into Mexico: The Diary of Susan Shelby Magoffin 1846–1847.* Lincoln: University of Nebraska.

Fisher, Leonard E. (1990). *The Oregon Trail.* New York: Holiday House.

Freedman, Russell. (1983). *Children of the Wild West.* New York: Clarion Books.

Fritz, Jean. (1986) . *Make Way for Sam Houston.* New York: Putnam.

Holliday, J. (1981). *The World Rushed In: The California Gold Rush.* New York: Simon & Schuster.

Holling, Clancy. (1942; renewed 1970). *Tree in the Trail.* Boston: Houghton Mifflin.

Hughes, Dean. (1986). *The Mormon Church: A Basic History.* Salt Lake City: Deseret Book Company.

Interact: Learning Through Involvement. Elementary Simulations Catalog. (1996). Lakeside, CA. (619) 448-1474.

Jakes, John. (1986). *Susanna of the Alamo.* San Diego: Hartcourt Brace Jovanovich.

Jeffers, Susan. (1991). *Brother Eagle, Sister Sky.* New York: Dial Books.

Jones, Hettie. (Ed.). (1971). *The Trees Stand Shining: Poetry of North American Indians.* New York: Dial Books.

Kurtz, Jane. (1990). *The Oregon Trail: Dangers and Dreams.* Grand Forks, ND: Roots and Wings Publishing.

Levine, Ellen. (1986). *If You Traveled West in a Covered Wagon.* New York: Scholastic.

MacLachlan, Patricia. (1985). *Sarah, Plain and Tall.* New York: Harper Collins.

McGovern, Ann. (1987). *The Defenders.* Scholastic.

McNeer, May. (1950; renewed 1977). *The California Goldrush.* New York: Random House.

Mitchell and Moehle. (1972). *Westward Expansion.* St. Louis, MO: Milliken Publishing.

National Council for Social Studies. (Bulletin 89, 1994). *Curriculum Standards for the Social Studies* (pp. 21–30). Washington, DC: Author.

O'Dell, Scott. (1970). *Sing down the Moon.* New York: Dell Publishing.

Pelz, Ruth. (1990). *Black Heroes of the Wild West.* Seattle, WA: Open Hand Publishing.

Petersen, David. (1991). *Sequoyah, Father of the Cherokee Alphabet*. Chicago: Childrens Press.

Ravitch, Diane. (Ed.). (1991). *The American Reader: Words That Moved a Nation*. New York: HarperPerennial.

Schlissel, Lillian. (1982). *Women's Diaries of the Westward Journey*. New York: Schocken Books.

Stein, R. Conrad. (1984). *The Story of the Oregon Trail*. Chicago: Childrens Press.

Stewart, George. (1954). *The Pioneers Go West*. New York: Random House.

Time-Life Books. (1976). *The Indians*. New York: Author.

Wilder, Laura Ingalls. (1932). *Little House in the Big Woods*. New York: Harper & Row.

Williams, Jeanne. (1992). *Trails of Tears*. Dallas: Hendrick-Long Publishing.

Quontamatteo, Nancy, et al. (1981). *The Gold Rush Era*. Jackson, CA: Conceptual Productions.

Audiovisual Resources

If These Walls Could Speak: Sutter's Fort. (Narrated by Vincent Price).

The Gold Rush and the 49ers. BFA.

Gone West. (Narrated by Alistair Cooke). Time-Life, 1973.

The Louisiana Purchase. MultiMedia Productions.

The Opening of the American West. United Learning, 1990.

The Santa Fe Trail. United Learning, 1991.

Seven Alone. (Directed by Earl Bellamy).

Westward Expansion: The Pioneer Challenge. Rainbow, 1992.

Computer Software

Lewis and Clark Stayed Home. MECC, 1991 (Apple).

The Oregon Trail: School Edition. MECC (Apple or IBM).

Santa Fe Trail. Educational Activities (Apple).

6 A Glimpse into the Rise of Civilizations through Myths and Legends

GRADE SIX UNIT
Focus: The Rise of Civilizations

LESSON TOPICS

- Myths and Legends: Ways of Thinking about Ancient Civilizations
- The Rise of Ancient Civilization: Mesopotamia
- Native Americans: Their Beliefs as Portrayed in Myths and Legends
- Dioramas: A Way to Illustrate Myths and Legends

Unit Rationale/Broad Goals

Unit Focus: *National Council for Social Studies Standards*

Strand 1. Social studies programs should include experiences that provide for the study of culture and cultural diversity.

Strand 10. Social studies programs should include experiences that provide for the study of ideals, principles, and practices of citizenship in a democratic republic (NCSS, 1994).

Along with archeology, much of what is known about the rise of civilization has been transmitted through myths and legends. These stories may or may not be true; however, literature reveals a great deal since early writers painted vivid pictures related to specific societies, their lives, and their beliefs. The literature coming out of the past sets the stage for a study that focuses on the way in which civilizations rose and the people who were responsible for their development.

As students study mythology and legends, they began to see geography and phenomena of nature as significant factors in the rise of early civilizations. In this unit a bridge is made from the earliest civilizations to later civilizations in the North American continent. The students are encouraged to become active participants as they focus on people and places, their everyday lives, their contributions, and their beliefs that are transmitted through literature.

This unit provides a glimpse into the past as the students develop time lines, become involved in research and writing projects, integrate art activities, and work cooperatively as they examine example early civilizations. Instructional strategies will include the use of audiovisual materials—such as videotapes, map activities, and technology—to enhance the learning. The ideas in this unit of study provide a direction for teachers as they investigate ways to explore ancient civilizations. The ideas presented are intended to be a framework that will guide the study of other great civilizations; however, the ideas presented will serve to provide meaning and elicit interest as they compare the early civilizations with the rise of later civilizations on the North American continent through myths and legends.

Lesson 1: Myths and Legends: Ways to Think about Ancient Civilizations

Time Frame: 1 to 2 days

Materials/Equipment: *Myths and Legends from around the World* (Shepard), a map of Mesopotamia for each student, a transparency made from the map of Mesopotamia, overhead projector, pens.

Broad Objective: The students will learn that myths and legends provide information about the rise of ancient civilizations.

Specific Objective: After listening to a myth related to natural phenomenon, the students will:

1. Develop a map of ancient Mesopotamia that illustrates the significance of geography, specifically water sources, in the rise of civilizations.

Anticipatory Set/Motivation: "Throughout time people have attempted to explain why the world is the way it is and how it originated. In past lessons we read verifiable stories about people, places, and events. Archaeologists and historians attempt to clarify the origin of human societies. However, in the distant past—before any sciences existed—the beginning of the world and societies were explained by myths and legends. Myths usually focus on some phenomenon of nature, the origin of man, or the customs, institutions, religious rites, and beliefs of people. Myths do not necessarily explain correctly what happened, yet they are one way of thinking about the past. This suggests that behind mythical explanations there are realities that cannot be seen and examined. Legends are stories handed down for generations that frequently evolved from a historical event that is not verifiable. I will read an example story that was passed on through the generations to explain the creation of the world."

Input: The teacher will read an excerpt from one of the many Native American tales. After reading and clustering ideas from the story on the board, the teacher will locate the tribe on a map and remind the students that this story originated in more recent times. "Today we are also going to read about people in ancient times. Our stories will begin with the people of Mesopotamia, who may have developed the first known civilization. Much of what we know about the Sumerian people of Mesopotamia is derived from myths and legends." The teacher will read a brief account titled "Heroes and Heroines" from the book *Myths and Legends*. (Write names of people and myths on the board.) "To set the stage for subsequent stories, we will develop a map to locate the ancient site of Mesopotamia, which lay between the Tigris and Euphrates Rivers in southwest Asia." The teacher will point out that this area is now known as Iraq. The surrounding landforms will be located on a large world map.

Modeling/Guided Practice/Independent Practice: Each student will be provided a map representing ancient Mesopotamia (see Figure 6.1). The *Children's*

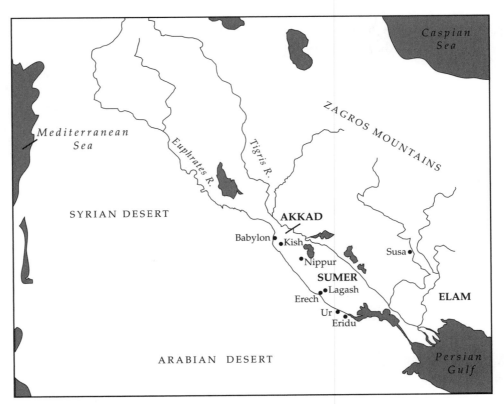

Source: Adapted from Mason (1994).

Figure 6.1   Ancient Mesopotamia

Atlas of Civilization (Mason, 1994) and the *Visual Dictionary of Ancient Civilization* (1994) are excellent resources that provide information to guide the development of student-made maps. The focus will be on the Tigris and Euphrates Rivers. The students will draw boundaries and indicate the areas in which the earliest cities are believed to have been established. This map will be completed independently by each student and placed in a folder that will be developed during the subsequent lessons in this unit. Those who finish early will be encouraged to create a cover picture for their folders.

Closure: The teacher will review the major map features and point out that this map will guide them in subsequent lessons as they learn more about the people of Mesopotamia and the area in which they lived. The students will be reminded that much of what is known about these people has been transmitted through myths and legends. The teacher will close this lesson by telling the students they will learn more the next day about ancient civilizations and Gilgamesh, who once ruled the ancient city of Uruk in Mesopotamia. As homework, they will be asked to find information about Gilgamesh that can be shared with the class.

Provide for Differences: Audio, visual, and kinesthetic activities have been included to actively involve the students. The interest eliciting mythical stories should motivate the students as they begin this journey into the past. The map will provide the necessary visual to focus the students and prepare them for future lessons. Students needing more help will be paired with others who can provide assistance. The students will be encouraged to illustrate their learning and thought in an artistic way by creating covers for their folders.

Lesson 2: The Rise of Ancient Civilization: Mesopotamia

Time Frame: 4 to 5 days

Materials/Equipment: *Gilgamesh the King* (Zeman), *Myths and Legends* (Shepard), Colliers Encyclopedia, *The Visual Dictionary of Ancient Civilization* (Eyewitness Visual Dictionaries), *The Children's Atlas of Civilizations* (Mason), *The Beginning of Civilization in Sumer: The Advent of Written Communication* (Social Studies School Service).

Broad Objective: The students will become aware of what is meant by *civilization*.

Specific Objective: After reading myths and legends as well as accounts provided by historians, groups of students will investigate Mesopotamia to gather data that indicates the existence of what is believed to be the first known civilization.

Anticipatory Set/Motivation: (This motivation will function as the transition into a group investigation project.) "In a prior lesson we read mythology about people from ancient civilization and their beliefs related to the origin of life. The stories set the stage for our research into the first known civilization, which rose in the area of present day Iraq. The area we will explore was called Mesopotamia. We read brief accounts of heroes and heroines that included Gilgamesh, who is believed to have lived in this area." (Elicit from the students any information they found related to Gilgamesh. This was homework assigned the previous day.) This information can be clustered on the board. Additional information will be added during the lesson development. An example cluster is shown in Figure 6.2.

"Today we will learn more the rise of civilization as we read about Gilgamesh and the Sumerians who lived in the area of Mesopotamia. This story is one of the earliest written stories in the world. Listen carefully about what it tells us about the values and beliefs that were held by many people in ancient times. These same values of courage, friendship, and peace are with us today."

The story "Gilgamesh" (from *Myths and Legends* [Shepard]) will be read. During and after the reading, the teacher will elicit student input and add to the cluster that was begun earlier. After the story is read, the teacher will ask questions related to the rise of civilization in the area of Mesopotamia. This leads into the subsequent lesson procedure.

Lesson Procedure (Group Investigation Model)

1. *Encounter Puzzling Situation:* "We have learned about people who lived during ancient times. Although these stories are considered to be myths, they do tell a great deal about the people, their beliefs, and the area in which they lived. These stories vary depending on the specific group of people who lived in each of the early civilizations. However, major questions remain to be

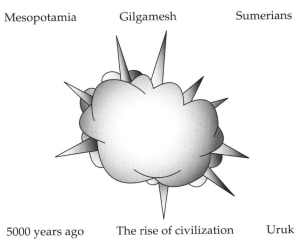

Mesopotamia   Gilgamesh   Sumerians

5000 years ago   The rise of civilization   Uruk

Figure 6.2   Mesopotamia Cluster

answered. For example: How do we know about these stories? What is a civilization? What conditions are necessary for the rise of civilization?"

2. *Explore Reactions to the Questions:* These questions prompt students to react. As the students react, the teacher draws attention to specific ideas. (The stories were told orally before writing was developed. Water was necessary for agriculture to develop. It was necessary to invent ways to survive in early civilization.) The students will be guided into noticing differences in what was thought to be needs in early civilizations. (Perhaps some may feel they do not know enough to determine how civilizations develop.) The teacher will draw attention to the need to research one early civilization as an example.

3. *Formulate Study Tasks and Organize for Study:* As the students become aware of the need to know more about early civilization, the teacher will guide them in structuring their research. Because it is believed the Sumerian people— who lived in the area of Mesopotamia—developed the first known civilization, the teacher will guide the students in formulating a study of this area and its people.

   Ideas will be elicited and written on the board by the teacher. The students will be reminded that although mythology and legends are about gods, goddesses, and kings, they also provide bits of evidence about early civilization. Later discoveries also provide clues related to the people, their beliefs, and the way in which they lived. The teacher will guide the students as they make a list of topics one would study to more clearly understand the concept of *civilization.* The suggested topics for study should include:

building of cities	inventions/science/technology
religious beliefs	development of writing
form of power/government	agriculture
family life	art forms

   The students who show interests in a specific topic will form a study group. The formation of additional groups of two to three students will be guided by the teacher to assure the inclusion of important topics. After each group is formed, the students will be guided into selecting a recorder and a spokesperson. Resources will be made available in the classroom, and suggestions will be provided for additional resources available in the school and local libraries.

4. *Independent and Group Study:* Each group will carry out its assignment. This will occur independently as well as in groups. The students will begin the research in school and continue as an homework assignment. Because this activity will take several days, on the first day each group will focus on formulating its research plan, provide specific student tasks, and plan for each participant's independent research task. The next day each group will coordinate the efforts of its members, and summarize the results of its investigation for the recorder and spokesperson.

5. *Analyze Progress and Process:* Each small group will report back to the larger group to inform other students of the progress each group made in its investigation. Groups will present their information in summary form and analyze their progress. The teacher will guide the groups in evaluating their

efforts and to help them determine if they have gathered accurate and meaningful information.

6. *Recycle Activity:* Students may have discovered evidence that they could not clearly depict in their selected topics. In that case, students might choose to investigate further to illustrate their topics more clearly. Their final research findings will be presented to the entire class.

Extended Activities

1. After each group presents its findings to the entire class, students will write their reports as though they were newspaper articles. Each summary will be attached to a bulletin board in a form that resembles the front page of a newspaper. The students will provide a name for the newspaper—such as *The Mesopotamian Daily News.*

2. An alternate form of presenting student findings could include the development of murals created by each group to illustrate its topic.

3. The students will construct a written and pictorial time line that indicates and illustrates the time frame in which the Sumerian culture lived, flourished, and died.

4. Computer software and videocassettes can be made available in the classroom to allow for other forms of research and reinforcement. The following can be obtained through Social Studies School Services, Culver City, CA, (800) 421-4246.

   Ancient Mesopotamia: This videocassette is an overview of the rise and fall of civilization in the Fertile Crescent. Focuses on inventions/farming and irrigation.

   Daily Life in the Ancient World: This videocassette will provide excellent information for those exploring daily life in early Mesopotamia.

   Rivers and Ancient Cultures: This computer software includes two Apple disks and a teacher guide. It focuses on the relationship of rivers and the rise of civilization.

   The Beginning of Civilization: The Advent of Written Communication: This is a series of lesson plans that includes illustrations and information about cuneiform writing as well as information related to ziggurat buildings.

Lesson 3: Native Americans: Their Beliefs as Portrayed in Myths and Legends

Time Frame: 3 to 4 days

Materials: *How We Saw the World* (Taylor), *Keepers of the Earth* (Caduto & Bruchac), *The Girl Who Loved Coyotes* (Wood), *Buffalo Dance* (Van Laan), *Star Boy* (Goble), *Turquoise Boy* (Cohlene), *The Legend of the Indian Paintbrush* (dePaola), *Dancing Drum* (Cohlene), *Arrow to the Sun* (McDermott), overhead projector, legend transparency, book paper, and art supplies for the story books.

Broad Objective: The students will understand that the beliefs of Native Americans were revealed through myths, legends, and stories.

Specific Objective: After reading myths, legends, and stories about early North American Indian tribes, small groups of students will summarize and illustrate selected stories that will be compiled into a class book.

Anticipatory Set (Motivation): "We have learned that stories about the people living in early civilizations provide insight about their lives and beliefs. Many of these stories attempted to explain natural phenomena. However, people in all areas of the world have tried to explain natural phenomena. The first story that we read in this unit of study was an attempt by the Maidu Indian tribe in Northern California to explain the creation of the earth. That story is only one of the stories that are as numerous as the people and varied as the geography in which they evolved. Diverse people expressed their beliefs through legends and myths, yet commonalities and differences exist between the stories told by the Sumerians and those passed on from generation to generation by the Native Americans. For example, both the Sumerians and the Native American tribes told stories to explain the creation of the world; however, many of the stories told by Native Americans reveal a deep respect for animals, Mother Nature, and human's relationship to nature. Listen to this story, told by the Navajos of Southwestern United States. Later we will summarize the message in this story."

Input/Modeling: Read the story "Four Winds: The Dine Story of Creation" (from *Keepers of the Earth* by Caduto & Bruchac). After reading the story, the teacher will elicit student ideas related to the message in the story. The teacher will guide the students as they develop a summary version of the story. An example will be provided as the teacher elicits ideas from the students and models the writing of the summary. The following example illustrates the written assignment for the subsequent group activity.

> Begochiddy designs the First World. The discontent and misdeeds of the other beings bring flight from the First World into the Second, Third, and finally the Fourth World. Begochiddy plants the Big Reed each time to carry everything from each world to the next. When Coyote, the human beings, and others reach the Fourth World, Begochiddy tells the human beings how to live right, to care for the plants, and to give thanks—for the Fourth World, our world of today, can also be destroyed by human beings (Taylor, *How We Saw the World*, p. 34).

Guided Practice: The teacher will read the story "How Thunder and Earthquake Made Ocean" (from *Keepers of the Earth* by Caduto & Bruchac, p. 93). The students will be provided time to write a brief summary. The teacher will elicit student responses and guide students in determining that the message focused on the importance of water. The ocean creatures come to live in the water as food for people. This immediate feedback will prepare students to write their own story summaries. Groups of three to four people will be provided a story that they will read and summarize. Possible choices are provided below:

Arrow to the Sun (McDermott)   *Dancing Drum* (Cohlene)
The Legend of the Indian Paintbrush (dePaola)   *Turquoise Boy* (Cohlene)
Star Boy (Goble)   *Buffalo Dance* (Van Laan)
The Girl Who Loved Coyotes (Wood)

Group Activity: The students will take turns reading portions of the story while the others take notes. After the story is completed, students will all provide input to write the final summary. When the summary is finished, students will illustrate their version of the story on scratch paper.

Closure: The teacher will ask for volunteers to share their stories. The next day, students will proofread, rewrite, and illustrate their stories. These stories will be combined and laminated to form a book of North American Indian stories.

Lesson Extension: The students might create Readers' Theater scripts based on the myths they read. The summaries and the actual legends or myths can be adapted to Readers' Theater scripts. These student adaptations of stories, legends or myths will add an element of realism in the presentation of their scripts to the other class members. "Weaving Readers' Theater and Nonfiction into the Curriculum" (Young & Vardell) provides an excellent model for the development of Readers' Theater in the classroom.

Lesson 4 : Dioramas: A Way to Illustrate Myths and Legends

Time Frame: 2 to 4 days

Materials/Equipment: *The Visual Dictionary of Ancient Civilization* (Eyewitness Visual Dictionaries), *Myths and Legends from Around the World* (Shepard), *The Children's Atlas of Civilizations* (Mason), *Plains Indian Diorama* (Kalmenoff). The resources will also include related Sumerian and Native American literature as well as historical accounts and resources depicting myths and legends about kings, goddesses, and gods. The following names are included as examples:

Enhil = king of heaven and
    earth
Nanna = moon god
King Gudea = a ruler of
    Lagash

Enki = god of water and wisdom
Nidaba = goddess of writing and
    accounts
Ur-Nammu = king noted for
    writing law codes

Broad Objective: The students will artistically represent their understanding of early civilizations by creating dioramas.

Specific Objective: After the teacher provides an example and describes the development of a diorama:

1. Small groups of students will develop dioramas to illustrate their understanding of a myth or legend they read during this unit of study.
2. Write stories to describe their dioramas.

Anticipatory Set (Motivation): The teacher will read excerpts from the Blackfoot legend, *Buffalo Dance* (Van Laan). The discussion will focus on the special bond between the buffalo and the Blackfoot people. The dance that is performed before and after the hunt is a way of showing respect to the buffalo. The teacher shows a model of a diorama illustrating the buffalo dance. (A diorama will be defined as a miniature three-dimensional scene depicting figures or scenery in a realistic way.)

Input/Modeling/Guided Practice: Directions and information will be provided that include:

1. The availability of appropriate related literature (the students will be reminded they can choose to depict either Sumerian or Native American stories).
2. Materials necessary for the dioramas (shoeboxes, larger cardboard boxes, student-constructed background scenery, and objects to place in the diorama).
3. Time frame in which students will construct the dioramas.

Group Activity: During the first session, the teacher will provide guidance to groups of students as they decide how they will illustrate selected myths or legends as well as the materials they may need to construct the dioramas. Group members will assign themselves tasks to be completed as homework. The construction of the dioramas can begin the next day. When they are finished, the students will write brief stories depicting their dioramas.

Unit Extensions

1. The dioramas and stories will be presented to the other class members and be put "on stage" in the classroom as evidence of their knowledge and completion of the study of early civilization through myths and legends.
2. Computer software can be made available to reinforce the study of early civilizations. Example: *Microsoft Ancient Lands*, Microsoft (Macintosh, Windows CD-ROM).
3. The students can be encouraged to read, compare, and contrast the myths

and legends of other early civilizations such as those from ancient Egypt and Greece.

4. After viewing the videocassette *Early Civilizations* (BFA Educational Media), the students can be asked to develop—in small groups—collages that depict the conditions that allowed civilizations to develop. The collages can include both pictures and words. *National Geographic* is an excellent resource for this activity.

Related Literature

Allan, Tony. (1993). *Pharaohs and Pyramids*. London: Usborne Publishing Ltd.

Bottero, Jean. (1992). *Mesopotamia*. Chicago: The University of Chicago Press.

Caduto, Michael J., & Bruchac, Joseph. (1989). *Keepers of the Earth*. Golden, CO: Fulgrum.

Cohen, Amy, L. (1993). *From Sea to Shining Sea: A Treasury of American Folklore and Folk Songs*. New York: Scholastic.

Cohlene, Terri. (1990). *Dancing Drum*. Mahwah, NJ: Watermill Press.

Cohlene, Terri. (1990). *Turquoise Boy*. Mahwah, NJ: Watermill Press.

dePaola, Tomie. (1988). *The Legend of the Indian Paintbrush*. New York: G.P. Putnam's Sons.

Eyewitness Visual Dictionaries. (1994). *The Visual Dictionary of Ancient Civilization*. New York: Dorling Kindersley Publishing.

Goble, Paul. (1983). *Star Boy*. New York: Macmillan.

Kalmenoff, Matthew. (1985). *Plains Indians Diorama*. Mineola, NY: Dover Publications.

Lattimore, Deborah N. (1992). *The Winged Cat: A Tale of Ancient Egypt*. Mexico: HarperCollins Publisher.

Lister, Robin. (1994). *The Odyssey*. New York: Kingfisher.

Mason, Anthony. (1994). *The Children's Atlas of Civilization*. Brookfield, CT: The Millbrook Press.

McDermott, Gerald. (1974). *Arrow to the Sun*. New York: Penguin Books.

National Council for Social Studies. (Bulletin 89, 1994). *National Standards for the Social Studies* (pp. 21–30). Washington, DC: Author.

Sabuda, Robert. (1994). *Tutankhamen's Gift*. New York: Macmillan.

Shepard, Sandra. (1995). *Myths and Legends from Around the World*. New York: Simon & Schuster Macmillan.

Taylor, D. J. (1993). *How We Saw the World*. Plattsburg, NY: Tundra Books.

U.S. News and World Report. (May, 1995). "Tales from the Crypt: Ramses the Great." *U.S. News and World Report, 118*(21), 52–60.

Van Laan, Nancy. (1993). *Buffalo Dance*. Boston: Little, Brown and Company.

Weatherill, Sue & Steve. (1995). *Hieroglyph It!* Hauppauge, NY: Barron's Educational Educational Series.

Wood, Marian. (1990). *Cultural Atlas for Young People: Ancient America*. New York: Facts on File.

Wood, Nancy. (1995). *The Girl Who Loved Coyotes*. New York: William Morrow and Company.

Young, Terrell, A. & Vardell, Sylvia. (February, 1993). "Weaving Readers Theater and non-fiction into the curriculum." *The Reading Teacher, 46*(5).

Zeman, Ludmila. (1992). *Gilgamesh the King*. Plattsburg, NY: Tundra Books.

Zeman, Ludmila. (1995). *The Last Quest of Gilgamesh*. Plattsburg, NY: Tundra Books.

Audiovisual Resources

Ancient Mesopotamia: This is an overview of the rise and fall of the civilization in the Fertile Crescent.

Daily Life in the Ancient World

Early Civilization, BFA Educational Media

Computer Software

River and Ancient Cultures: Includes two Apple disks and a teacher's guide. The focus is on the relationship between rivers and the rise of civilizations.

Microsoft Ancient Lands: Microsoft (Macintosh, Windows CD-ROM).

Social Studies
Instruction
Incorporating the
Language Arts

Index